Creating History Papers

Creating History Papers

By **Bradford C. Brown**

Published by the
American Historical Association
400 A Street, SE
Washington, DC 20003
www.historians.org

About the Author: Bradford C. Brown, PhD, has taught courses in History, Western Civilization, and Sociology at Bradley University since 1996. His research focuses on the meaning of kingship in the political culture of revolutionary France in the early nineteenth century.

AHA Editors: Allen Mikaelian, Liz Townsend

Cover and Layout Design: Chris Hale

Cover Photo: Sydney Harbour Bridge by the author

Acknowledgements: Many thanks to my colleagues—including Rob Townsend and the anonymous reviewers at AHA—for support and practical suggestions, to my teachers for inspiration, and to all my students for showing me what works. Thanks, too, to Courtney Wiersema for permission to adapt parts of her paper.

Published in 2013 by the American Historical Association. As publisher, the American Historical Association does not adopt official views on any field of history and does not necessarily agree or disagree with the views expressed in this book.

Library of Congress Cataloging-in-Publication Data:

Brown, Bradford C.

Creating history papers / by Bradford C. Brown.

pages cm

Includes bibliographical references and index.

ISBN 978-0-87229-204-8 (alk. paper)

1. History—Methodology. 2. History—Research. 3. Academic writing. I. Title.

D16.B874 2013   907.2—dc23   2013030854

Table of Contents

I: Reflecting

1. Creating History

What does the word *history* mean?

Ask anyone for the obvious answers. They will remind you that history is a record of websites surfed. Or history is "baggage"—the backstory that every individual brings to a new relationship ("Careful, he has a history"). It describes the losers, the outpaced, and outmoded ("Dude, you are so history!"). Or history is that section in the bookstore, next to the biographies. Everyone also knows that it is a kind of class you take in school. (If you are lucky, you get a marvelous teacher who inspires with stories and creative assignments; if unlucky, you suffer in Mr. Gradgrind's room cramming endless lists of facts and dates.) And all these contemporary uses derive from the same basic meaning that history is the past—everything that has ever happened before now . . . and now . . . and now as the edge of the self-erasing present glides onward and consciousness becomes memory.

Ask *historians* the same question though and the answers will be different. For professionals, history is a personal problem: how to live in the present while thinking deeply about the past. It is a matter not merely of training, association, and employment, but of curiosity, effort, and risk, of lengthy investigations, hazarded interpretations, sharp debate, and public controversy. So they will tell you that history is an extended discussion, a conversation among the living about the dead. It is a social search for true knowledge and consequently entails the ethical responsibilities that all human interactions oblige. It is more a written conversation than a spoken one because writing offers the hope of addressing complexity with precision. So history is composition, too—not just the mountains of words already stacked but also the ongoing challenge of shaping new arguments in order to express new insights, persuade skeptics, and inform the uninitiated. And, as with all writing, it is about craft and technique as well as description and logic, about authorial skills as well as authoritative research. For practitioners then the answer is that history is identity *and* ethics, art *and* science, creativity *and* responsibility.

This answer may seem surprising. In an age when rebels are celebrated as heroes, any restraint appears to oppose the freedom of imagination and originality. But this is a mistake, a modern blindness. Necessity fosters invention; confrontation with the unavoidable sparks creativity. Artists, writers, scientists, engineers—all of us, really—must cope opportunistically with the constraints of models and materials as well as the limits of personal ability. According to Picasso, even abstract art (seemingly the most liberated form of self-expression) is itself grounded in the experience of reality. So when historians wrestle to find, understand, present, and discuss the results of their research, they too are engaged in acts of creation.

This reference guide is designed to address the "hows" of history papers. It lays out technical information to aid students engaged in the process of researching, writing, and documenting. But the "rules" laid down in these pages are articulated in the service of historical research and not for their own sake. So in addition to the toolkit, this guide includes occasional spurs to reflection. From the start, as you make your own way forward as a historian, consider some alternative answers to the question "what is history?" Remember, each of us, beginning and advanced students alike, contribute a small but meaningful part to creating history.

Further Reading

Mihaly Czikszentmihalyi, *Creativity: Flow and the Psychology of Discovery and Invention* (HarperCollins, 1996).

Davor Dzalto, "Creation vs. Techne: The Inner Conflict of Art," in *Analecta Husserliana*, vol. CVI: *Art Inspiring Transmutations of Life*, ed. P. Trutty-Coohill (Springer, 2010), 199-212.

Carl R. Hausman, "Creativity: Conceptual and Historical Overview," in *Encyclopedia of Aesthetics*, ed. M. Kelly (Oxford: Oxford University Press, 1998), 453-56.

Christian Zervos, "Conversation avec Picasso," *Cahiers d'Art* 10 (1935) in *Letters of the Great Artists, vol. 2: from Blake to Pollock*, ed. R. Friedenthal, trans. E. A. Evans (London: Thames and Hudson, 1963), 256-60.

Andrew Robinson, *Sudden Genius? The Gradual Path to Creative Breakthroughs* (Oxford University Press, 2010).

2. What Is History?

Honest history is the weapon of freedom.
—Arthur M. Schlesinger, Jr.

History is a needle / for putting men asleep / anointed with the poison / Of all they want to keep.
—Leonard Cohen

History is a set of lies agreed upon.
—Napoleon

History is not history unless it is the truth.
—Abraham Lincoln

The best history is . . . like the art of Rembrandt; it casts a vivid light on certain selected causes . . . which were best and greatest; it leaves all the rest in shadow and unseen.
—Walter Bagehot

History, real solemn history, I cannot be interested in. . . . I read it a little as a duty; but it tells me nothing that does not either vex or weary me. The quarrels of popes and kings, with wars and pestilences in every page; the men all so good for nothing and hardly any women at all.
—Jane Austen

There is properly no history, only biography.
—Ralph Waldo Emerson

Historical study is not the study of the past but the study of present traces of the past.
—G. R. Elton

History is a damn dim candle over a damn dark abyss.
—W. Stull Holt

The writing of history reflects the interests, predilections, and even prejudices of a given generation.
—John Hope Franklin

We are ourselves history and share the responsibility for world history and our position in it.
—Hermann Hesse

History at its best is vicarious experience.
—Edmund S. Morgan

History is, strictly speaking, the study of questions. . . .
—W. H. Auden

History is who we are and why we are the way we are.
—David McCullough

History is the effort to explain the unexplainable out of anxiety. The ancients told religious stories, we tell historical stories.
—William H. McNeill

Mankind are so much the same, in all times and places, that history informs us of nothing new or strange. . . . Its chief use is only to discover the constant and universal principles of human nature.
—David Hume

The past does not repeat itself, but it rhymes.
—Mark Twain

There is a history in all men's lives, / Figuring the natures of the times deceased, / The which observed, a man may prophesy, / With a near aim, of the main chance of things / As yet not come to life.
—William Shakespeare

History is Philosophy teaching by examples.
—Thucydides

History is one damn thing after another.
—Anonymous

History, n. an account mostly false, of events mostly unimportant, which are brought about by rulers mostly knaves and soldiers mostly fools.
—Ambrose Bierce

The principal office of history I take to be this: to preserve the memory of virtuous actions and to prevent evil words and deeds by instilling the fear of an infamous reputation with posterity.
—Tacitus

History is nothing but a pack of tricks that we play upon the dead.
—Voltaire

Voltaire to the contrary, history is a bag of tricks which the dead have played upon historians.
—Lynn White, Jr.

There is no history, only histories.
—Karl Popper

The one duty we owe to history is to rewrite it.
—Oscar Wilde

The history of the world / is hearsay. Hear it. / The whole truth / is unspeakable / and nothing but the truth / is a lie.
—Lee Robinson

By liberalizing the mind, by deepening the sympathies, by fortifying the will, history enables us to control, not society, but ourselves . . . it prepares us to live more humanely in the present and to meet rather than to foretell the future.
—Carl Becker

Properly speaking, history is nothing but the crimes and misfortunes of the human race.
—Pierre Bayle

All true histories contain instruction.
—Anne Bronte

History is the transformation of tumultuous conquerors into silent footnotes.
—Paul Eldridge

History does not refer merely, or even principally, to the past. On the contrary, the great force of history comes from the fact that we carry it within us, are unconsciously controlled by it in many ways and history is literally present in all that we do.
—James Baldwin

History is a relay of revolutions.
—Saul Alinsky

Americans see history as a straight line and themselves standing at the cutting edge of it as representatives for all mankind. They believe in the future as if it were a religion; they believe that there is nothing they cannot accomplish, that solutions wait somewhere for all problems, like brides.
—Frances Fitzgerald

To study history means submitting to chaos and nevertheless retaining faith in order and meaning. It is a very serious task . . . and possibly a tragic one.
—Hermann Hesse

The history of the world is the world's court of justice.
—F. von Schiller

History . . . is a nightmare from which I am trying to awake."
—James Joyce

We learn from history that we never learn anything from history.
—G.W.F. Hegel

Histories make men wise.
—Francis Bacon

History is a bucket of ashes.
—Carl Sandburg

History is the self-consciousness of humanity.
—J.G. Droysen

History is an argument without end.
—Peter Geyl

History is indeed the witness of the times, the light of truth.
—Cicero

If you don't look back, / the future never happens.
—Rita Dove

See also "Quotes about History," ed. F. M. Szasz, *History News Network* (2005), www.hnn.us/articles/1328.html.

II: Researching

This section provides concise directions for history students undertaking a research project. It offers neither an adequate description of how historians always work nor a comprehensive prescription for how they should. Instead, it simplifies the usual steps of the process and offers practical tips for beginners along the way.

But this section also seeks to provoke reflection about the sources of excellence in historical practice. If virtues are qualities that we admire in others, and by ethics we mean principles of laudable behavior, then what are the exemplary intellectual virtues and best ethical practices to which contemporary historians can agree to aspire? This big question—too grand, perhaps, for a space so small—at least restores attention to the issue of ends, to which the problem of means must always return.

See also 35. For Researching *under* VII: Internet Resources *page 73.*

2. Asking Questions

2a. The Virtue of Curiosity

> *"Curiouser and curiouser!" Cried Alice . . . "Now I'm opening out like the largest telescope that ever was!"*
> —Charles Dodgson

"Curiosity," according to Samuel Johnson, "is one of the permanent and certain characteristics of a vigorous intellect." Yet people are not always curious, preferring pat answers, regular patterns, and comfortable routines. Loose ends are unsettling. (Is this a reason to write history—to feel better about the chaotic present by organizing the past?) What is worse, we seem to become less curious with age. But curiosity can be cultivated. Raising questions can become a habit, one query leading to the next. Asking good questions requires practice and reveals something about ourselves. The Duke de Lévis considered it better to "judge others by their questions rather than by their answers."

Sources: Lewis Carroll, *Alice's Adventures in Wonderland*, ch 2.; S. Johnson, *Rambler*, no. 103 (12 March 1751); P.-M.-G. de Lévis, *Maximes et réflexions* (1808), no. xvii.

2.1: Think about Topics

Occasionally a research project begins with a topic in hand. Mostly they must be found.

- **Multiple Topics**—there are countless possible topics. You will be astonished at the diversity of subjects selected by classmates. But students worry too much about finding a perfect topic. Instead, try to come up with three topics (or more). You can settle on one later.

- **Topics that Find You**—good topics are often connected to personal interests. So ask yourself some questions. What ten terms define who you are? Where have you traveled or where would you like to go? What kinds of people do you admire? What is your favorite history book or movie?

- **Topics in the Air**—lots of good topics are interesting because they are a part of our lives today. Look around and listen to what people are talking about now. What issues are in the news, on the covers of magazines, or trending in social media? What controversies—in politics, music, on the playing field—are important to you?

- **Uncovered Topics**—often the best topics grow out of historical research. Questions pop up because something in the reading does not make sense or simply catches your eye. So read something short: a capsule biography, a famous historical document, a section of a textbook. Find an illustration of an artwork or an artifact to examine closely.

- **Assigned Topics**—ask your instructor for a couple of topics to choose between.

2.2: Narrow the Topics

Topics are almost always too broad at the beginning. Refining a research topic is necessary because the world of sources is wide and you have only so much time for any one project. Do not worry about being too specific, you can always expand your topic later. Here are three quick ways to narrow a topic:

- **Limit the Scope**—focus your topic geographically, by time period, or by groups of people. Restrict the topic by looking at only one country or region, one short span of time, one organization, or even one or two individuals.

- **Choose an Angle**—include a theoretical perspective to frame or guide your work. Emphasize one aspect of identity such as class, gender, race, ethnicity, or nationality. Approach the problem from the standpoint of a particular kind of history: intellectual, environmental, cultural, social, labor, military, or political. Or think about using environmental, feminist, Marxist, psychoanalytical, or postmodern theory. But remember that the theory invoked in the topic should be part of the historical question, and that it should help to clarify rather than obscure your argument.

- **Pick Among Possible Sources**—restrict yourself from the start to a range of sources, such as books by two authors, readings in an anthology, a set of newspapers.

2.3: Choose One Topic

There are many reasons for preferring one topic over the others. The most important considerations are Interest, Originality, and Feasibility. The topic should be exciting because the research will require a lot of energy. It should make clear your contribution to existing knowledge. And it should be doable given your skills and the available resources. For these reasons, the final choice probably should take place after a period of deliberation and the early exploration of potential sources.

2.4: Compose a Research Question

Restating a refined topic as a question can be harder than it seems. So spend some time on this.

- **Types of Historical Questions**—some questions cannot be answered by historical research. So it may help to note that historical questions tend to focus on three types of problems. The comparison of similarities and differences between two moments in the past is a problem of *Continuity or Change over Time*. An assessment of the array of significant factors and circumstances that influenced individuals and events in the past is a problem of *Context*. The understanding of the ideas, states of mind, and experiences of people in the past is a problem of *Meaning*.

- **Writing the Question**—research begins with the question. So write yours out as a single sentence ending with a question mark. Be prepared to rewrite the question as your research progresses.

- **Working Thesis Statements**—the point of research is to investigate difficult questions without obvious answers. But it is never too early to think about possible answers or theses. A thesis is an argumentative answer to a question. Try writing out one or more working theses.

- **Research Proposal (Prospectus)**—the research question and a tentative answer are the foundation of a prospectus—that is, a formal proposal of planned research. A prospectus should also include a brief introduction to the topic, a review of the secondary literature, a working bibliography, an indication of the nature and scope of the primary sources to be consulted, a timeline for the project, and possibly a budget (*See* 3.2: Organize the Search, *page 13*).

2b. Ethics of an Open Mind

Why is an open mind better than a closed one?

Is doubt better than belief?

Doesn't certainty bring happiness?

Is anticipating the probability of error more useful? more truthful? more ethical?

Is it possible to keep an open mind? How?

3. Finding Sources

3a. The Virtue of Diligence

Learning is not attained by chance, it must be sought for with ardor and attended to with diligence.

—Abigail Adams

Oddly, there seems to be no established word in our language for the quality of being excellent at, or simply disposed toward, detection. This is particularly strange given detection's close relation to the long-valued abilities of hunting and gathering—to *track down* and *ferret out*, to *glean* and *unearth*. But, in popular culture at least, Sherlock Holmes epitomizes this virtue. Although treasured more for his quick conclusions than hard work, Holmes regards this as a misperception of his methods. In *A Study in Scarlet*, he remarks to Watson: "They say that genius is an infinite capacity for taking pains," before concluding "It's a very bad definition, but it does apply to detective work." *Diligence* derives from an old Roman word and means something akin to this notion of a "capacity for taking pains." It is determination and heedfulness, persistence and care, doggedness and accuracy all combined toward the completion of a task.

Sources: Abigail Adams to John Quincy Adams (20 March and 8 May 1780), in *Adams Family Correspondence*, ed. L. H. Butterfield and M. Friedlaender (Cambridge: Belknap Press, 1973), 3:313; Arthur Conan Doyle, *A Study in Scarlet* (Modern Library, 2003 [1887]), 29.

3.1: Think about Sources

A typology of sources is commonplace in introductions to historical method, but rarely is the logic for these distinctions spelled out. A researcher in the early stages of a project should think broadly about the variety of potential sources.

Primary, Secondary, & Tertiary Sources—sources are roughly sorted into categories by their *proximity to the topic of analysis*. Most commonly the distance indicated is chronological, but the remove could also be geographical, social, or cultural. *Primary Sources* are closest to the topic (the artifacts and documents produced by participants or near observers such as letters, diaries, interviews, and other writings from the time). *Secondary Sources* are accounts from a greater distance which rely on primary sources (for example, books or articles by later historians). *Tertiary Sources* build on secondary sources (such as encyclopedia entries or textbooks).

This classification places value on the hard work of tracking down and interpreting primary sources, encourages the development of original arguments, enables a more sophisticated criticism of other secondary sources, and emphasizes professional expertise. But limitations and ambiguities abound in this system (a topic explored further in "Examining Sources" below). Consider, for example, the following potential sources. Should they be considered primary or secondary?

◆ a 1775 newspaper article about a riot written by a journalist who interviewed participants and shopkeepers.

◆ an 1831 description of slave family-life in a letter of a slave owner.

◆ an 1863 battle described in a veteran's autobiography published in 1928.

◆ a diary entry from 1900 on the use of English slang among the ship's crew by an American traveling in China.

Media—another way to sort out sources is by their physical characteristics. *Artifacts* are objects made by humans—tools, clothing, buildings, and the like—and are referred to collectively as the *material culture* of a society or era. *Images* are artifacts that can be further subdivided by artistic techniques and material composition—with sculpture, drawing, painting, and photography as basic categories. (*Maps* are an important hybrid between images and writing.) Written sources come in a myriad of styles and formats, which may explain the tendency among historians to call all sources *documents* or *texts*. *Manuscript* sources are written by hand and different handwriting styles can be distinguished as *scripts*. *Typescript* sources are produced mechanically. The complex history of publishing over the last five hundred years has produced many other technical terms for sources—such as *incunabula* (printed works up to the year 1500), *broadsides* (large printed sheets often with popular songs or descriptions of sensational crimes), and *blogs* (online journals).

Common Usage—sources are also commonly divided on the basis of varying criteria. So, for example, diaries and letters differ by format and purpose even if they say similar things. All *periodicals* are published at set intervals but we distinguish between *newspapers* and *magazines* on the basis of paper quality and between magazines and *journals* on the basis of expertise and audience. *Monographs* are long arguments on one topic (most often by a single author) published as a book and *articles* are shorter arguments. An *anthology* is a collection of articles published as a book. Digital publication has started to blur the lines between these categories.

Location—artifacts can be found in historic buildings and museums, or circulating as antiques. Documents are typically housed in the library collections and archives of colleges and universities, local historical societies, regional and national governments. But they can also be ferreted out in the private collections of enthusiasts or in the forgotten corners of family attics. Sometimes documents molder in place for a millennium, sometimes they migrate to the most unexpected places. The memoir of a German soldier who served in Napoleon's army in Russia turned up in a Kansas farmhouse. One of Leonardo da Vinci's notebooks became a prized possession of Bill Gates.

Recognizing Scholarly Secondary Sources—nearly anyone with a computer can publish on the internet and if you have money to spend and an axe to grind you too can publish a book. This makes the question of authority particularly important, namely "why should I trust this author?" Keep your eye out for the following signs of serious scholarship:

◆   *Look for Citations*—scholarly works in history always include the careful citation of sources in notes and bibliographies.

◆   *Notice the Publisher*—university presses are not the only publishers of scholarship, but this is their main purpose. Look up publishers you do not recognize.

◆   *Read Acknowledgements, Prefaces, and Author Notes*—scholars routinely recognize professional colleagues who have helped in creating the work as well as institutions that have provided financial grants to aid research. Such acknowledgements can provide clues about the author's connection to a scholarly community.

◆   *Find Out More about Authors*—a little research often provides more information about the education and career of the authors you consult.

3.2: Organize the Search

The search for sources is determined more by the perseverance of the researcher than by the number of available sources. Finding sources is a continuous process with a big push at the beginning followed by frequent updates. Organize the search with open-ended files that address the questions of *how* the search will move forward and *what* you are looking for.

Establish a Schedule—budget time for research and writing by scheduling time every day and every week. Set weekly and monthly goals. Leave adequate time for writing and re-writing.

Keep a Research Register—list search terms as well as sites and locations that you have searched or plan to search. A register might look like this:

I. Search Terms and Subject Headings

II. Online Sites

    1. Search Engines

    2. Gateways, Portals, and Subject Directories

    3. Databases

    4. Catalogs

III. Locations (Libraries, Archives, & Museums)

Build a Working Bibliography—organize all the relevant sources on your topic into a list. The bibliography should include all sources to which you have found references even if you have yet to track them down. Subdivide your working bibliography and try to find materials for each of the following subsections:

I. Reference Sources

    A. Websites

    B. Books

    C. Articles & Chapters

II. Scholarly Secondary Sources

    A. Monographs

    B. Anthologies

    C. Articles

    D. Book Reviews

III. Primary Sources

    A. Archives and Collections

    B. Images and Other Artifacts

    C. Written Documents (Published & Unpublished)

3.3: Find Reference Sources Online

Use general reference sources to gain an overview of your topic. For better or worse, the convenience of the internet makes it the starting point for twenty-first-century research. But, effective online research requires more than finding your way to *Wikipedia*. Challenge yourself to become an expert at internet searching. *For some internet resources, see 35.2: General Reference, page 73.*

Search Engines—there are many search engines and the better ones have different strengths. Learn to use more than one. Try metasearch engines that request information from multiple engines simultaneously, or try specialized search engines specific to a field of study or

2b. TIP: Subject Headings

Note headings for each book you find in library catalogs, since the new terms may lead you to other relevant topics and still more sources.

region of the world. *For more suggestions, see* 35.10: Search Engines, *page 81.*

Search Terms—search engines interpret each symbol or word entered with precision, not imagination; you must therefore understand the logic of their results.

◆ Use keywords specific to your topic:

Change the order of keywords

Use longer and alternative versions

Put specific phrases in quotation marks

Keep a list of terms and phrases to reuse in other databases

◆ Use basic operator symbols in front of keywords:

+ or AND means include only sites with this term

- or NOT means exclude this term

~ means include synonyms of the term

OR between keywords means include sites with either term

◆ Use advanced search pages:

Limit your searches by time period, number ranges, occurrences (where terms appear: titles, urls, abstracts, etc.), domains, etc.

Gateways, Portals, & Subject Directories—these are all terms for websites that organize edited lists of links to high-quality internet resources. Gateways and the like are of increasing value to researchers because they save time by collating earlier searches. *For suggestions, see* 35.3: Gateways, Portals, & Subject Directories, *page 74.*

Websites & Webpages—websites are interlinked collections of webpages. They vary enormously in quality and the researcher must often hunt a bit to find information about authors, sponsors, and latest updates. *See* 35.1: Evaluating Internet Resources, *page 73.*

3.4: Find the Reference Sections of the Library

Every university library has at least two areas devoted to tertiary sources:

Library Websites—reference works are increasingly available online through subscriptions. The library home page will direct you to internet reference sources that may only be accessible through this site.

Reference Stacks—reference sources in the library usually do not circulate (i.e., they cannot be checked out) and are shelved separately from circulating materials. In this section of the library you will find encyclopedias, atlases, and dictionaries as well as scholarly reference works on many topics.

> ### 2c. TIP: Talk to Librarians
>
> Reference librarians can point you to finding aids that list useful publications by topic. They can also guide you to sections of the library you may not have considered. They are often sitting at a desk waiting for questions but they answer email too.

3.5: Find Scholarly Secondary Sources

Bound volumes of journals, monographs, and edited works comprise the vast bulk of holdings in a college or university library.

Look for Monographs and Anthologies in Library Catalogs—most everyone is familiar with finding books using the online catalog databases that have almost entirely replaced card catalogs, but here are some more advanced techniques.

- *Keyword Searches*—use a variety of words and phrases. *See* Search Terms *under* 3.2: Organize the Search, *on page 13.*

- *Subject Searches*—based on Library of Congress Subject Headings (LCSH). These subject headings are called authorities. You can also search them in the big red published directories that are prominently shelved in most reference sections. Or you can search the listings online at: authorities.loc.gov.

> ### 2d. TIP: Browse Shelves
>
> When tracking down books in the library, remember to browse titles on nearby shelves—you will build your bibliography and gain a larger sense of related fields of research.

- *Author Searches*—look up other books and articles by authors of useful sources.

- *Call Numbers*—every cataloged item in a library has a call number. U.S. research libraries use Library of Congress Classification (LCC) in which books on history are often (but not always) shelved under C (Auxiliary Sciences of History), D (Old World History), or E & F (History of the Americas). Pay attention to call numbers and learn the LCC. *See also* 35.6: Library Classification Guides, *page 79.*

- *Use Interlibrary Loan (ILL)*—you may have privileges at other libraries through your own. Use ILL to request books and articles from off-campus locations. Or visit those other libraries in person.

- *Find More Online Catalogs*—many libraries are directly searchable. *See* 35.5: Library Catalogs, *page 78.*

- *Consult Digitized Library Collections*—full- and partial-text books are increasingly available online. *See* Portals, Collections, & Digital Libraries *under* 35.4: Primary Sources, *page 76.*

Look for Articles & Book Reviews in Online Databases—many databases index articles in magazines and journals. Each database is limited in the number of periodicals it indexes and the period of time it covers. *See* 35.7: Databases for Articles, Dissertations, & More, *page 79.*

- *History Journals*—you can search for scholarly articles in history journals by using the advanced search pages in databases like JSTOR and Project Muse. Pay attention to the date limitations for the articles included in these databases. *See also* 35.8: History Journals Directories, *page 80.*

- *Book Reviews*—add reviews of major books on your topic to the working bibliography. They are a useful guide to controversy in the field as well as to other titles and authors.

2e. TIP: Scan References

Expand your bibliography quickly by reading the notes and bibliographies of more recent articles and books.

3.6: **Find Primary Sources**

Relevant artifacts and documents vary by topic and are only uncovered through diligence. *Review the basic types of sources in* 2.1: Think about Sources, *starting on page 11.* Here are a few places to begin the search.

- **Quoted Primary Sources**—often the first clue to the existence of a primary source is a reference in a secondary source. Pay close attention to the citations of key evidence in books and articles.

- **Online Collections**—use search engines and gateways to track down digitized primary sources. *See* 35.4: Primary Sources, *page 75.*

3f. **TIP: Network**

For extended projects, contact scholars, librarians, and archivists in the field after you have exhausted the obvious online resources and talked to local experts.

- **Published Collections**—use library catalogs to find published primary sources either in the original editions or in edited collections.

- **Archives and Special Collections**—look for collections at libraries and museums and by searching databases of archives. *See* 35.9: Archives & Museums, *page 80.*

3g. **Ethics of Investigation**

Why do we value hard work? Does it shape character or show it? Is it a mug's game?

How much work is enough? Do we need to turn over every stone? Or just be honest about the number of stones turned?

Is a little research done well better than much done poorly? How can we tell the difference?

Why are we obligated to be accurate? Who cares and what do we owe them?

Does a stitch in time save nine? Is carefulness more efficient?

Is there pleasure in the chase? In the puzzle? In the process and the product?

Who are we that we push ourselves so?

4. Examining Sources

4a. The Virtue of Judgment

In a good history the judgment must be eminent, because the goodness consisteth in the method, in the truth and in the choice of the actions that are most profitable to be known.

—Thomas Hobbes

Criticism is the general art of comprehending, analyzing, and evaluating human actions and creations. All readers are critics. The best of them not only articulate their own immediate emotional and intellectual responses to a work but also seek a deeper understanding of it. They learn to appreciate its purpose, to dissect its structure, and to estimate its place in the world. In this process of negotiating complexities, wisdom as well as science guides the encounter of a critic with a text. "True scholarship," according to James Russell Lowell, "consists in knowing not what things exist, but what they mean; it is not memory but judgment." Judgment in this sense is the critical faculty. It is the ability to distinguish, discern, and grasp. In an earlier age, it was wit; in our more practical age, it is acumen and savvy. It is the ability to stand in the middle of things—somewhere between faith and cynicism (as Mason Cooley once put it)—and still make good sense.

Sources: T. Hobbes, *Leviathan*, ch 8.; J. R. Lowell, "The First Need of American Culture," Harvard Crimson (4 May 1894) quoted in Ferris Greenslet, *James Russell Lowell: His Life and Work* (Houghton Mifflin, 1905), 130, Google Books; M. Cooley, *City Aphorisms*, ninth selection (1992).

4.1: Read Thoughtfully

Understanding the meaning of any source is a process of interpretation. Even the simplest text or artifact can have hidden complexities. Every source requires careful examination.

Basic Comprehension—reading a primary source often starts by decoding its language, idiom, and style. Beyond language study and other major disciplines, there are a number of auxiliary sciences devoted to understanding particular kinds of sources. For example:

- *Epigraphy*, the study of inscriptions
- *Genealogy*, the study of family records
- *Historical Metrology*, the study of weights, measures, and exchange rates

- *Numismatics*, the study of currency, especially coins and medals
- *Paleography*, the study of handwriting
- *Sigillography*, the study of seals on documents

Active Reading—reading is never a passive process of absorbing knowledge. The examination of sources requires an especially energetic approach. Read vigorously!

- *Needles in Haystacks*—if a project is based on culling small bits of information from large amounts of material, then begin with the index or a quick scan of the relevant sections. At one extreme, historians who use quantitative methods (sometimes called cliometrics) may be looking for isolated facts to count.

- *Close Reading*—at other times reading must slow to a crawl as the researcher tries to understand the meaning of key passages or even a single word by re-reading the text, looking up definitions in older dictionaries, and puzzling out meaning through contextualization.

- *Seeing the Argument*—active reading also means figuring out the relationship between parts of a source and the whole.

  Look for explicit *summaries of the argument* (sometimes in the form of thesis statements and topic sentences), or reconstruct the implicit arguments of each part of the source.

  Keep one eye on the *organizational logic* of the source (sometimes helpfully expressed in a table of contents). Stop occasionally to think about why a passage is included at a given point.

Critical Evaluation—after reading the source, assess its usefulness. *See also* 35.1: Evaluating Internet Resources, *page 73, and* Using & Evaluating Primary Sources *under* 35.4: Primary Sources, *page 75.*

- *Perspective & Bias*—historical research depends on an evaluation of the potential distortions in every source. Error, narrow vision, and illogic cloud the products of the human mind. Beyond these unintentional failings, sources are shaped by the arts of deception, misdirection, and imagination. Perspective and bias are terms (of sympathy and disapproval, respectively) that signal these distortions.

- *Key Questions*—in the process of evaluating sources, consider the following questions:

  When and where was the work created?
  Who created it?

What was the creator's background?

What were the purposes of the work?

Who were its audiences?

What factors in that time and place—such as social conflicts, cultural attitudes, economic incentives—might have influenced the creator?

Are there signs of bias in the work?

Are there omissions and silences about important topics?

4.2: Take Notes

Understanding a series of sources and remembering their relevance to a longer research project requires extensive, organized note-taking.

Basic Source Notes—take these notes for every source you encounter.

◆ *Bibliographic Information*—The first step when examining a new source is to copy down the relevant information for the bibliography. In general, this means noting the author, title, and other basic information (*see* IV. Documenting, *page* 47). For unpublished sources and artifacts, notes should include information about the collection and any relevant classification.

◆ *Page Numbers*—use a consistent system for noting page numbers (or other helpful divisions in a source) for every note you take. Be careful to note the divisions between pages, too. One method is to add a slash in brackets [*/*] or a slash with the new page number [*/***322**].

◆ *Outlining Sources*—building a basic outline of the source is a useful step towards understanding its arguments and briefly summarizing its details.

◆ *Paraphrase and Summary*—work on rewriting short passages in your own words (paraphrase) and condensing longer sections in your own words (summary). Be extremely careful to avoid transferring the same words from the source into your notes. If you cannot think of a different word or phrase then simply add quotation marks to indicate that they come directly from the source.

◆ *Quotation*—treat all quotations with care and precision. Everything within the quotation marks must accurately mirror the original. Do not change punctuation. Do not correct misspellings. Omit unnecessary material with ellipses.

Highlighting & Marginalia—should you mark-up personal copies of texts? Two schools of thought disagree on the issue (although digitization of texts may make this debate obsolete.)

♦ *For*—underlining, highlighting, and writing in the margins are all forms of active reading. They allow for a quick and effective way of noting relevant passages and jotting down reader comments.

♦ *Against*—highlighting can become an excuse for not reading carefully and avoiding the work of interpreting the meaning of the source for the project. Paraphrasing, summarizing, and transcribing notes from a source encourage a more active engagement with the source and better preparation for writing. Underlining and marginalia often get in the way of a fresh re-reading of a source because what seems relevant for one project may not be the same for the next. Finally, this way of taking notes seems to encourage the distressing tendency to write in library books.

Personal Notes—keep a separate notebook or file in which to jot down ideas as they occur to you while reading.

Note Systems—there are many different ways to keep notes organized as you read through sources and then rearrange them for the writing stage. The choice of a note system reflects the nature of the project, available resources, and individual preferences. Before you begin, consider these basic options:

♦ *Bound Notebooks*—a bare-bones option. Advantages: page size and binding. Disadvantages: difficult to rearrange for writing.

♦ *Note Cards*—the classic approach. Advantages: encourages brief paraphrases, summaries, and quotations; ease of rearranging notes for writing. Disadvantages: limited space on a card; requires card files to organize; slippery devils.

- *Word-Processing Software*—a more powerful and versatile option. Advantages: unlimited size and number of files; allows copying between files; allows searching among many files. Disadvantages: requires computer; not designed for research notes.

- *Note-Taking Software*—the ultimate in professionalism. Advantages: designed for research note-taking; automated citation functions. Disadvantages: cost (although some are free); time for learning the system. *For current options, see* 35.11: Note-taking Software Reviews, *page 81.*

4c. Ethics of Detachment

Do historians resemble lawyers in their pursuit of the truth?

Should we favor sympathy like defense attorneys or suspicion like prosecutors?

Or should we be impartial like judges and jurors?

Should we distrust arguments expressed passionately?

Should we try to see the world through another's eyes?

Is objectivity attainable or are we stuck in our own skins?

5. Building an Argument

5a. The Virtue of Deliberation

When you approach a problem, strip yourself of preconceived opinions and prejudice, assemble and learn the facts of the situation, make the decision which seems to you to be the most honest and then stick to it.

—Chester Bowles

Advocacy is of real value for historians, and assertiveness, courage, and passion all have their place in making arguments. But qualified conclusions achieved after long study merit a deeper respect. The ability to "entertain a thought without accepting it" as a "mark of an educated mind" is an idea often attributed to Aristotle. The quotation is probably mistranslated, but Aristotle certainly believed in the concept of deliberative excellence—that is, the capacity to listen to different opinions, to weigh reasons, and to engage in mature reflection. John Stuart Mill also praised this virtue. In the midst of his own stirring defense of deliberation, he pointed out that the famous Roman lawyer Cicero "always studied his adversary's case with as great, if not with still greater, intensity than even his own." Mill concluded that "all who study any subject in order to arrive at the truth" should follow Cicero's example and added: "He who knows only his own side of the case, knows little of that."

Sources: Bowles, attributed; J. McGinness, "Aristotle & Accuracy," 22 Feb. 2009, *Denouement*, publicnoises.blogspot.com/2009/02/aristotle-and-accuracy.html; J. S. Mill, *On Liberty*, ed. S. Collini (Cambridge University Press, 1989 [1859]), 38.

5.1: Form an Interpretation

The purpose of a research project is to arrive at a considered and persuasive answer to the question.

Reflection during Research—think about how you will answer the research question even as you track down sources and take notes.

Ending the Research Phase—give yourself time to think and write well before the due date. Remember that more focused research may be necessary in the writing phase to bolster your emerging argument.

Thinking through Outlines—map out the paper's argument by drafting outlines. For longer papers you will need two: a *brief outline* of the overall organization and a *detailed outline* that includes each paragraph. Revise these outlines as you write.

Rewrite the Research Question—this is an essential step toward formulating a clear, direct, and argumentative thesis statement. You may need to revise the question more than once as you think through the outline of your argument.

5.2: Write the Paper

Writing the paper should build on earlier writing: source notes, jottings about inspired ideas, the working bibliography, and the draft outlines. As you construct your argument, consider how you will address the following issues.

Selection—to write, is to choose, as the saying has it. Good arguments are tightly focused on only the evidence and analysis necessary to make the case. Not everything that you learn in your research belongs in the finished paper. Use the outlining process to identify the key sections of your argument. Strengthen those sections and cut out anything that is irrelevant.

Counter-Evidence—consider carefully any evidence that seems to contradict your argument. Addressing this evidence directly strengthens your case.

Specific Modes of Argument—although the entire paper should be one interconnected argument, there are a variety of forms that the argument can take. At times, the argument may need to marshal precise historical details. The explanation of a particular thing (such as a book, an institution, a ritual, or a theory) in depth is called an *Exposition*. An account of the way things were experienced (looked, sounded, felt, smelled, or tasted) is called a *Description*. A chronological presentation of events is called a *Narrative*. These modes are most effective when used infrequently and to a particular end.

5.3: Revise the Paper

Budget time to re-write the paper and hone the argument.

Compare Paper & Outline—revising the outline one last time based on the first complete draft of the paper will provide another opportunity for thinking through the logic of the argument.

5b. Ethics of Audience

What responsibility do authors owe their readers?

Should we report the failings, lapses, and limitations of our research alongside our conclusions?

Is honesty really its own reward? Might it have other compensations?

Is it possible to be too honest?

Who do you imagine in your audience?

Is it fair to assume that your readers are educated? That they know the subject? That they understand technical or big words?

Is clarity an ethical imperative?

Is writing more a matter of freedom or responsibility?

Is it expression or communication?

Is writing a personal activity or a social one?

III: Writing

How to Look Like You Know What You Are Talking About might be a good title for a style guide. Style is about appearance and, as everyone knows, form matters. Design catches the eye and craftsmanship commands respect. This section offers a guide for students who already know how to write but wish to become more proficient. It describes the customary expectations of history instructors and anticipates common problems in undergraduate papers. It summarizes some of the general advice of the *Chicago Manual of Style* and other guides. It highlights useful things to know about formal writing and reduces style to a set of formal rules of expression. But writing style—what Samuel Wesley once called "the dress of thought"—can also be defined as a quality of individuality or of excellence. After trying on these clothes, you may want to expand your wardrobe. *See also* 36: For Writing, *under* VII: Internet Resources, *page 83.*

6. Preparing to Write

6.1: Gather Basic Materials

Access to a computer, word processing software, a printer, and a stapler is necessary. Having a dictionary, a thesaurus, and a style guide close to hand is highly recommended. *See* 35.2: General Reference, *page 73, and* 36.1: Guides to Composition, *page 83.*

6.2: Consult with the Instructor

Start early and ask questions concerning preferences for writing style and formatting, and about the assignment.

6.3: Take Accurate Notes

Write down quotations and ideas as you read, carefully noting sources and page numbers.

6.4: Format the Paper

If there are no other guidelines, use these standard recommendations. *See* 30. Sample First Page & Bibliography, *page 68.*

Control the Margins—one-inch margins on all four sides.

Add a Heading—single-space the heading (paper title, course number and title, author's name, and date) in the top left corner of page one, inside the margins. Title pages are unnecessary for short papers.

Add Page Numbers—number every page (except the first) in the upper-right corner in the header.

Format Paragraphs—indent the first line of each paragraph 0.25 inch with a tab. Use 12-point font, preferably Times New Roman. Double-space everything (except the heading). Justify the left margin only.

Bind the Paper—staple the upper-left corner.

---

7. Writing Persuasively

7.1: Think about Your Audience

Imagine an educated but easily distracted audience, familiar with the topic but skeptical of your point of view.

Keep Your Readers' Attention—choose adjectives and verbs carefully. Keep sentences as short as possible and break up a series of long sentences with a short one. Connect sentences and paragraphs with transitional words and phrases.

Avoid Biased and Offensive Language—do not use *man* or *mankind, he* or *his* when you mean everyone.

7.2: Focus on Evidence Analysis

Emphasize Primary Sources

Use Scholarly Secondary Sources

Acknowledge Opposing Arguments—explain evidence that appears to contradict your argument.

But Avoid:

- *Quoting reference sources*—consult *Wikipedia* and other encyclopedias (and list these sources in your bibliography), but do not expect to impress anyone with this kind of research.

American Historical Association

- *Stating personal opinions.*

- *Long summaries of events and descriptions.*

- *Comparisons to current topics or events*—unless this is part of the assignment.

7.3: Pay Attention to Time

Write in the Past Tense—except when discussing the work of people living in the present.

Think about Chronology—indicate important dates when relevant. Avoid skipping back and forth in time. Be clear about days, months, and years when narrating events.

7.4: Pay Attention to People

Name and introduce the individuals who are connected to the topic and events you are discussing. Authors are people too, so introduce them as well if you cite them.

7.5: Write Simply and Directly

Find words that convey your meaning precisely. Pick short words over long ones. Focus each sentence on one point. Use adequate and expressive punctuation.

7.6: Write Formally

Do Not Use Contractions

Do Not Use Slang Terms or Conversational Phrases

Avoid the First Person (*I, we, me, my, mine, ours*)—although some assignments may require it and some instructors may tolerate its limited use.

8. Organizing Content

8.1: Outline the Argument

Write a working outline and revise it as you write. Often overlooked by students, outlining is the most efficient way to think through the organizational logic of the argument. Include a thesis statement and topic sentences in your outline. *See* 8a. Outlining, *page 30.*

8.2: Open the Argument in the Introductory Paragraph

Consider writing the introductory paragraph last, after having written the rest of the paper.

Opening Line—begin with an arresting sentence that will interest readers.

◆ Describe an odd fact, a provocative image, a compelling event. State an outrageous proposition, a paradox, a problem. Quote a pithy or funny line.

◆ Do not begin with a broad generalization.

Explanation of the Topic—present the topic, problem, or specific question that the paper addresses.

Thesis Statement—summarize the main point of the argument.

◆ The thesis should answer the whole question. (If the assignment is not already posed as a question, restate it as one.)

◆ A strong thesis is specific and argumentative.

◆ Strong theses include reasons for the answer and often are structured as "this because of that."

8.3: Build Supporting Paragraphs

Topic Sentence—include a statement of the main point of the paragraph, connecting the paragraph to the overall argument.

Evidence—a strong paragraph usually contains two or more pieces of evidence.

Explanations—connect the evidence and the topic sentence.

Transitions—transitional words or phrases link sentences and transitional sentences link paragraphs.

8a. Outlining

Divide the levels of organization and indent sublevels. Indicate both level and order with numbers or letters. Here is a typical progression of numbers and letters to indicate different levels.

I. A. 1. a. (1) (a) i) a)

Use a pilcrow (¶) to indicate a paragraph, a section sign (§) for sections, and bullet points (•) to separate items in a list.

8.4: Conclude the Argument

A concluding section or paragraph should bring the argument to a close without repeating earlier statements. Consider looking beyond the immediate topic to explain the broader significance of the argument or extrapolate its implications. The last sentence can be as important as the first one. End with an anecdote, a paradox, a rhetorical question, a reflection, an arresting image, or simply a powerful restatement of the thesis.

8b. Transitions

These basic categories and related words can be useful in thinking about how to connect ideas:

comparison—also, similarly, likewise, again, in comparison

contrast—on the one hand, on the other hand, although, nevertheless, despite, still, yet, regardless, at the same time, nonetheless, notwithstanding, whereas, but, however, on the contrary, in spite of, in contrast

addition—also, in addition, moreover, furthermore, too, besides

repetition—in other words, once again, to repeat

examples—for instance, specifically, particularly, such as, namely, for example

sequence—first, second . . . , next, subsequently, later, last, ultimately, finally

causation—consequently, as a result, because, accordingly, thus, since, therefore

time—next, later, after, meanwhile, while, immediately, earlier, shortly, in the future, subsequently, soon, since, as long as, at that time

space—next to, above, behind, beyond, between, here, there, opposite, to the right, in the background, over, under

concession—of course, naturally, granted, it is true that, certainly, admittedly

summary—on the whole, to sum up, in short, therefore, in summary

conclusion—as a result, as the data show, in conclusion, for this reason

Adapted and expanded from M. L. Rampolla, *A Pocket Guide to Writing in History*, 6th ed., (Bedford/St. Martin's, 2001), 56; and C. M. Anson et al., *The Longman Pocket Writer's Companion* (Pearson Longman, 2006), 13.

9. Integrating Evidence

9.1: Introduce the Source

Avoid dropping evidence into the argument without introduction. Acknowledge the source and context of the evidence with a *signal phrase* identifying the author, speaker, or title. Cite the source in a footnote when it is first introduced.

9a. Signal Phrases

A signal phrase alerts the reader to the source of the evidence by mentioning the author or title. Most signal phrases come before the evidence, but experiment by adding one in the middle of a quotation or even at the end. Observe how other writers insert signal phrases. Do not refer to page numbers in the signal phrase or text, leave them for the footnote. Mix up your verbs, too. Instead of "The author *says*. . .," try one of the following:

accept	claim	deride	insist	relate
acknowledge	clarify	describe	instruct	remark
add	comment	disagree	lament	report
admit	compare	disclose	maintain	respond
advise	complain	dispute	mention	reveal
advocate	concede	dissent	note	show
affirm	conclude	divulge	object	speculate
agree	concur	elucidate	observe	
allege	condemn	emphasize	plead	state
analyze	confirm	endorse	point out	stress
announce	consider	exclaim	predict	suggest
argue	contend	explain	proclaim	suppose
ask	declare	find	propose	testify
assert	defend	grant	protest	warn
assess	demand	hint	reason	wavers
avow	demur	hold	record	wonder
believe	deny	illustrate	refute	write
bemoan	deplore	imply	reject	

Adapted and expanded from D. Hacker, *A Pocket Style Manual*, 4th ed. (Bedford/St. Martin's, 2004), 120; and J. E. Aaron, *The Little, Brown Essential Handbook*, 5th ed. (Pearson Longman, 2006), 132.

9.2: **Present the Evidence**

Summaries, Paraphrases, & Quotations present textual evidence

◆ a *summary* condenses a long section of text into a sentence or two of your own words.

◆ a *paraphrase* rewrites a short section of text in your own words.

◆ a *quotation* exactly reproduces a passage of text between double quotation marks (" ").

Illustrations (or visuals) present evidence in visual formats, *see the box* 9b. Illustrations *below.*

9.3: **Quote Concisely**

Quote only essential words or passages by selecting the key idea and paraphrasing the rest. Integrate short quotations within the syntax of your own sentences or attach them to your sentences with punctuation (usually, commas or colons). When possible, avoid using quotations longer than four standard lines.

9.4: **Quote Precisely**

Every letter, space, and punctuation placed within the quotation marks must accurately reproduce the original source. Do not use quotation marks for indirect quotations—that is, paraphrasing someone else's words. Use quotation marks for words used ironically or with reservations. Use italics for technical terms or words as words.

9b. **Illustrations**

Visuals strengthen papers when carefully chosen and integrated with the argument; but too many oversized or irrelevant illustrations can be distracting and unhelpful.

Visuals are either *tables* or *figures* (the latter meaning drawings, images, maps, charts, and graphs). Each illustration should be labeled and numbered (for example, **Table 2.** or **Figure 5.**), and then captioned with an explanatory phrase or sentence. Cite the source or sources for the illustration with a footnote at the end of the caption [*often this will follow model* 29a: Source Quoted in Another Source, *page 66*].

9.5: Pay Attention to Quotation Punctuation

Double Quotations Marks—look like this: " "

Single Quotation Marks—look like this: ' '

Quotation Marks inside Quotation Marks—use single quotation marks for quotations within quotations. Use double quotation marks for a quotation within a quotation within a quotation! (Outside the U.S., other English-speaking cultures reverse this order, preferring to start off quotes with single quotation marks.)

Ellipses—an ellipsis looks like this: . . .

Brackets—look like this [ ]. Use brackets around words inserted into a quotation. Do this infrequently to clarify the meaning or to blend the quotation with the structure of a longer sentence.

Punctuation at the End of Quotations—In common usage, periods and commas are placed *inside* the final quotation marks, while other final punctuation are left *outside*, unless they belong to the original source. (An emerging trend in scholarly usage prefers to put all punctuation that does not derive from the original source outside the final quotation marks.)

9.6: Note Changes or Unusual Elements in Quotations

Emphasis—call attention to particular words in a quotation by setting them in italics, and then put (*emphasis added*) in normal font after the final quotation marks. If the italics are in the original, follow the quotation with (*emphasis in original*) in normal font.

Omitted words—An ellipsis in a quotation should be followed by (*ellipsis in original*) in normal font.

Sic—The Latin word *sic* may be placed within brackets in a quotation to signal an apparent error in the original, but this is not necessary when there are multiple errors and is rarely used anymore.

9.7: **Present Long (or Block) Quotations Differently**

Quotations longer than four standard lines should be set apart by (1) starting the quotation on a new line; (2) leaving off the quotation marks; and (3) indenting the whole quotation 0.5 inches from both the left and right margins. Use italics only for short quotations at the beginning of a paper (aka an *epigraph*)

9.8: **Cite the Source of the Evidence**

See IV: Documenting *on page 47, and* V: Examples of Source Citation *on page 59.*

Use Footnotes—cite all information when introduced and where relevant. *See* 17. Footnotes *on page 52.*

- Superscript footnote numbers are usually placed after the final punctuation in the relevant sentence or paragraph. Unless necessary for precision, footnote numbers should not be placed in the middle of a sentence.

- Quotations end with a period or other punctuation, followed by quotation marks and then by the footnote number.

- One footnote can include more than one source, so only one number is necessary at the end of a sentence or paragraph.

- Format each footnote reference precisely. *See* 17c. Differences between Footnote & Bibliographic Entries, *page 54.*

- The first citation of a source in the footnotes should be complete; subsequent citations to the same source should be shortened.

Add a Bibliography

- Begin at the top of a separate sheet and list all of the materials consulted in the process of preparing the paper—even those sources not used. *See* 30. Sample First Page & Bibliography, *page 68.*

- Format each bibliographic reference precisely. *See* 17c. Differences between Footnote & Bibliographic Entries, *page 54.*

9.9: **Explain the Relevance of the Evidence**

State your interpretation of the evidence as your reader might not read the quotation or paraphrase in the same way. Connect the evidence to the paragraph's topic sentence.

10. Understanding Plagiarism

10.1: Definition

Plagiarism (from the Latin word *plagiare*, meaning "to steal") is presenting someone else's words, ideas, or work without clearly acknowledging the original source.

10.2: Examples

Common forms of plagiarism include:

Incomplete Paraphrasing—you must change all the words in a paraphrase.

Missing Quotation Marks—you must put quotation marks around all words that come from the original source.

Missing Footnotes—you must cite a source for all paraphrased and quoted information.

Missing Source for an Illustration—you must cite a source for all visuals.

10.3: Penalties

Appropriate penalties for cases of plagiarism include papers earning zero credit and students receiving a failing course grade. Students might be asked to rewrite all or part of the paper on the same topic or a new one. Plagiarism cases are reported to department chairs and campus authorities.

10.4: Avoiding Plagiarism

Take Careful Notes—as you take notes, always write out complete source citations, add page numbers or web addresses, and double-check the accuracy of quotations.

10a. Thinking About Ethics

In one sense, *ethics* means the established standards of conduct, or rules for right action, governing a profession. (See, for example, the American Historical Association's *Statement on Standards of Professional Conduct*.)

But ethics is also a subject for public debate and personal reflection. What is right and wrong? What are the rules? How do we know? Who are our role models?

Consider the following questions: Is history a science that conducts research on humans? Do historians have ethical responsibilities to the people they study? To the people who read their work? To themselves? What are those obligations?

Next consider the oath below. Does it sound reasonable? Is it useful? Should it be longer? Say the oath aloud. Does speaking it feel different from reading it?

The Historian's Oath

"In seeking truth and understanding, I will be thorough in research, cautious in interpretation, and clear in argument."

Study the Proper Forms—learn the rules for source citation and follow them precisely.

Cite Sources Immediately—write your bibliography first; then acknowledge your sources in signal phrases and footnotes as you write. Do not wait to add your citations until the whole paper is finished.

Proofread All Paraphrases—double check the original source to avoid unintentional quotation.

Ask Questions!—consult your instructor about any remaining uncertainties well before turning in the paper.

11. Recognizing Common Errors

11.1: Titles and other Emphasized Words

Longer Works in Italics (or underlined)

- books, pamphlets, journals, magazines, newspapers, and websites
- plays, movies, tv, and radio shows
- artworks, such as sculpture and paintings
- uncommon foreign language words and phrases (but not familiar ones)
- names of ships, planes, trains, and spacecraft (but not types)
- scientific names for animals and plants (but not common ones)

Shorter & Unpublished Works in Quotation Marks

- articles
- chapters
- sections
- lectures
- short poems
- songs

Exceptions—capitalize but do not underline or italicize the titles of

- sacred books
- political and legal documents
- musical compositions identified by form, number, and key
- titles of publication series

Capitalize Specific Terms

- individuals, relatives, fictitious names, epithets, and job titles before proper nouns
- places, parts of the world, buildings, monuments
- nationalities, ethnic groups, languages (but related terms based on color, size, or colloquial usage are not capitalized)
- time periods, seasons, holidays, months, days of the week
- religions, scriptures, followers, sacred terms
- organizations, institutions, associations, and members
- historical periods, events, documents
- rebellions and revolutions
- military forces, wars, battles
- vehicles, ships, aircraft, spacecraft
- social and cultural movements, and artistic styles
- companies, trademarks
- scientific, technical, and medical terms
- academic departments and courses
- proper adjectives (adjectives based on the name of people, places, and things)

Do Not Capitalize Terms for Parts of a Book—*part, section, chapter, act, scene*

Capitalize Some Words in Titles, Subtitles, & Sections—capitalize first, last, and all principal words, but do not capitalize articles, prepositions, or coordinating conjuctions (such as and, but, or, so).

11.3: **Abbreviations**

Avoid using abbreviations for all but the most familiar personal titles, government agencies, corporations, and countries. To abbreviate a term used frequently in your paper, introduce the abbreviation in parentheses after using the full term for the first time, and use the abbreviation consistently thereafter.

Latin Terms & Abbreviations

These terms and abbreviations are rarely used outside of notes and some are now outdated.

c. or ca. *circa* (approximately), use before a date to indicate imprecision

cf. *confer* (compare), use before a counter-example

e.g. *exempli gratia* (for example), use before an example

et al. *et alii* (and other people), indicates additional authors

etc. *et cetera* (and the rest)

et seq. *et sequens* (and the following), use before many examples

fl. *floruit* (flourished), use to indicate when a person or thing was active

Ibid. *ibidem* (same thing), indicates the same source from the previous footnote

id. *idem* (same person), indicates the same author as the previous footnote

i.a. *inter alia* (among other things), use to cite one example of many

i.e. *id est* (that is), use before an explanation

  infra (below), indicates a subsequent footnote

loc. cit. *loco citato* (in the place cited), indicates the same source and page number from a previous footnote

N.B. *nota bene* (note well), use before an important cautionary statement

  sic (thus), use in brackets within a quotation to note an apparent mistake in the original source

op. cit. *opus citatum* (the work cited), indicates a work in an earlier footnote

  pace (by leave of), use before naming someone or a group who would disagree with the statement

  passim (here and there), use after a range of page numbers

  qua (as, in the capacity of)

  supra (above), indicates a previous footnote

q.v. *quod vide* (which see), use before a cross-reference; plural *quae vide* (qq. v.)

s.v. *sub verbo* (under the word), use before the title of an article in a source arranged alphabetically

vs. or v. *versus* (against)

viz *videlicet* (namely), use before a specification

11b. Roman Numerals

1	I
2	II
3	III
4	IV
5	V
6	VI
7	VII
8	VIII
9	IX
10	X
20	XX
30	XXX
40	XL
50	L
60	LX
70	LXX
80	LXXX
90	XC
100	C
200	CC
300	CCC
400	CD
500	D
600	DC
700	DCC
800	DCC
900	CM

See the pattern?
What letter means
one thousand?

11.4: Numbers

Spell out whole numbers that can be expressed in one or two words, as well as any number at the beginning of a sentence, **except** when the number is

- a date [*see* 11.5: Time Measurements, *below*]
- part of a percentage (add "percent" not %)
- a technical quantity followed by an abbreviation or a symbol
- part of a book
- one of many numbers in a sentence
- compared to other larger numbers
- part of a name (for names followed by numbers, such as Louis XIV, use capital roman numerals without punctuation).

Hyphenate numbers from twenty-one to ninety-nine.

11.5: Time Measurements

Time of Day

- Spell out times of day to the quarter hour, but use numerals for all other times or to emphasize exactness.
- Write a.m. and p.m. (for *ante* and *post meridiem*).
- Write noon or midnight, or 12:00 m. (*meridies*) for noon.

Dates

- Use cardinal numbers for dates even when they are pronounced as ordinals: so write 5 May, not May 5th.

- Prefer 31 May 1926 (Day Month Year) to May 31, 1926 (Month Day, Year).

- Spell out dates as ordinal numbers when the month is not given ("on the twentieth").

- Do not abbreviate days of the week or months of the year, except in footnotes.

Decades

- Write sixties or 1750s, not '60s and not 1750's.

Centuries

- Spell out centuries without capitals.

- As an adjective, a century is hyphenated; as a noun it is not *(nineteenth-century utopia* but *bohemians in the twentieth century)*.

Eras

- Capitalize abbreviations such as CE "common era" and BCE "before the common era" (which have largely replaced their equivalents AD, *anno Domini* and BC, "before Christ"). Using small capitals and periods is an acceptable older style.

- Era abbreviations come after the date, except put AD before the date.

11.6: Apostrophes

An apostrophe indicates that a noun possesses something or marks omitted letters as in contractions.

- Do not use contractions in formal papers.

- Do not use apostrophes to make plurals, including plural numbers, letters, abbreviations, and words-as-words.

- Add -'s to show possession for nouns that are singular and do not end in -s.

- Add just an apostrophe to show possession for nouns that are plural or end in -s.

11.7: Habits to Avoid

Repetition

♦ *Repeated Words*: use a synonym instead of the same word twice in connected sentences.

♦ *Too Many Colons*: One colon or semi-colon per paragraph is usually enough.

♦ *Multiple Negatives*: watch for more than one *no, not, nor* (or prefixes *un-* and *mis-*).

♦ *Clichés*

Vagueness & Unsupported Claims

♦ *Vague Words*, such as: *major, totally, good, great, very, really, a lot.* Replace others: *factor, aspect, situation, type, kind, stuff, thing, deal with.*

♦ *Wordy Phrases*, such as: as *a matter of fact, due to the fact that, in terms of, it seems that.*

♦ *Slashes*: choose between two words rather than joining them with a slash.

♦ *Vast Claims*, such as: *clearly, definitely, absolutely, obviously.*

Pompous Language

◆ *Technical Terms and Jargon*: avoid these if you can, but define and explain those that are essential to the subject.

◆ *"Creeping Nounism"*: Write about action through verbs rather than nouns. Watch out for strings of nouns and nouns that e n d in *–ion*.

11.8: Simple Word Errors to Correct

Affect & Effect

◆ *Affect* is (most often) a verb meaning "to influence." *Effect* is (most often) a noun meaning "result." But *effect* is also a verb meaning "to bring about" and *affect* a noun meaning "feeling or emotion."

Cite & Site

◆ A site is a place, to cite means to quote or mention.

Its & It's

◆ *Its* is the possessive form, *it's* is the contraction for *it is*.

Lead & Led

◆ *Lead* is a metal; *led* is the past form of the verb *to lead*.

Lose & Loose

◆ *Lose* is a verb meaning to misplace or the opposite of to win. *Loose* is an adjective meaning not securely fastened. You can lose a loose tooth, but not the reverse.

Novel & Book

◆ A *novel* is a longer work of fiction, but not all books are novels; some are even non-fiction.

Than & Then

◆ use *than* when making comparisons; *then* when discussing time.

11e. Hyphens & Dashes (and Parentheses)

Hyphens (-) are used to combine words and separate non-inclusive numbers (such as phone numbers).

The *en dash* is slightly longer (–). It means *through* when used with inclusive dates or numbers (such as July 27–29, or pp. 42–45). Hyphens are commonly used instead of en dashes.

The *em dash*, often just called the dash, is the longest (—). It is used in sentences to create a stronger break than a comma or to introduce a list. It can be used in pairs, like parentheses, or alone to separate a clause at the end of a sentence. If you cannot figure out how to create a dash, then two hyphens (--) will suffice. (When printing was done by hand, en and em dashes were the width of a typesetter's N and M.)

Parentheses and dashes emphasize additional information in a sentence. Use parentheses for clarifications, examples, tangential remarks, or to introduce abbreviations and acronyms. Use dashes sparingly to add emphasis, to set off a list, or to introduce a surprise, a shift in tone, or a final thought.

Do not put spaces on either side of hyphens or dashes.

---

12. Writing Checklist

12.1: Thesis

Where is the thesis statement?

Is the thesis specific? Is it debatable?

12.2: Supporting Paragraphs

What is the topic sentence?

Does the topic sentence cover the meaning of all the sentences in the paragraph?

Does the paragraph include evidence for all the key points?

12.3: Quotations

Is this quotation introduced with a signal phrase?

Could this quotation be shortened?

Is this quotation cited with a separate note?

Have you explained your interpretation of the quotation?

12.4: Footnotes & Bibliographic Citations

Is this the proper form?

Are the citations different for the notes and bibliographic entries?

Is the first note citation complete and are subsequent notes shortened?

12.5: Common Errors, Informalities, & Annoyances

Use a spell-checker to spot misspelled words.

Use a search command, like "find," to eliminate common mistakes

◆ Offensive Language: *man, mankind, he, his*

◆ Informality
  contractions
  first person: *I, we, me, my, mine, ours*

◆ Vagueness, Wordiness, Unsupported Claims
  very, major, great, totally, good, great, really, a lot
  factor, aspect, situation, type, kind, stuff, thing
  there is/are/were, it is; deal with
  as a matter of fact, due to the fact that, in terms of
  clearly, definitely, absolutely, and *obviously*

◆ Commonly misused words
  affect/effect
  cite/site
  its/it's
  lead/led
  lose/loose
  novel/book
  than/then

Re-read for common problems

◆ Titles and Emphasized Words

◆ Abbreviations & Numbers

◆ Time Measurements

◆ Misplaced Apostrophes

Creating History Papers   **45**

IV: Documenting

Source citations are both sign and symptom of professional history. To the uncritical reader, notes and bibliographies are an annoyance; to the scholar, they are indispensable. Styles of documenting sources have developed incrementally over centuries. From the house rules of book publishers and academic journals, citation style guides have gradually evolved to become more universal and adaptable, even if they continue to appear baffling and esoteric. This section aims to demystify footnotes and bibliographies for history students by offering a guide to the logic behind source citations as well as the process of adding notes and building a bibliography. It also presents a simplified system of documentation for student history papers.

In the architecture of historical citation, form does not wholly follow function—delighting traditionalists and distressing modernists. For the former, there are more intricacies of source citation to explore in the pages of the latest edition of *The Chicago Manual of Style*. For the latter, there is the assurance that the digital revolution has only just begun. *See also* 37. For Documenting *under* VI: Internet Resources, *page 84.*

---

13. General Requirements

13.1: Give Essential Information Accurately

All source citations should provide precise information about (1) authors, (2) titles, and (3) other basic facts that will allow readers to locate the sources so indicated.

13.2: Use Prescribed Forms Consistently

The form of each citation is determined by conventions in the classification of sources. Footnotes and bibliographic entries are similar in content, but different in form.

---

14. Authorship

14.1: Give the Author's Name

List the name as it appears in the source.

Add a space between initials.

Do not include degrees (e.g., *M.D.* or *Ph.D.*), job titles, ascriptions (e.g., Saint or Queen), or affiliations.

When possible, put the author's real name in brackets after a false name or pseudonym.

If the author is not known, start with the title. Do not use "Anonymous" or "Anon."

Multiple Authors' names should be listed in the order in which they appear in the source.

14.2: Corporate Authors

Use the organization name instead of a personal author, if no author is listed.

14.3: Credit Editors and Translators

When no author is listed, cite the editor or translator before the title. When a single author is listed (or is obvious), the name of the editor or translator comes after the title. Treat other roles (such as "with Introduction and Notes by") as subsumed by "editor."

15. Title

15.1: Write Titles in Headline Style

Use normal font, capitalizing first letters. Capitalize first, last, and all principal words but not articles, prepositions, or coordinating conjunctions (*and, but, or, so*).

15.2: Separate Subtitles

Use a colon for the first subtitle and semicolons for additional subtitles. Where there is other punctuation, such as exclamation or question marks, no colons are needed.

15.3: Emphasize Titles & Subtitles

Long works are italicized. Do not use underlining. Short works are set within double quotation marks. Titles within titles are set off with either further quotation marks (single or double as appropriate) or by the absence of italics.

15.4: Leave out Series Titles & Series Editors**

15.5: Note Volume Numbers

The volume number should follow the title. Volume numbers are often part of subtitles.

15.6: List Titles for Parts of Books

If it has a separate title, list that part of the book in quotation marks (or in italics if the part is a longer work like a poem or play), followed by the word "in" and the book's full title. If the part of the book is generic (an introduction, preface, afterword, or the like), it should not be set in quotation marks.

15.7: Generic Titles

For material without a title (*Letters to the Editor, Reviews, Editorials*), generic titles must be added.

15a. ** Note Differences from Chicago Style

Since the publication of its first edition in 1906, *The Chicago Manual of Style* (aka Chicago Style, CMS, or CMOS) has become the standard style guide for historians in the U.S. But style is never static or universal. Many academic journals and publishers still retain their own distinctive preferences. Evolving tastes and changing technologies continue to prompt new questions about writing and new editions of the CMS (*see* 37.2 CMS, *page 84*). The guidelines offered here, anticipating student needs and future trends, sometimes alter or simplify current Chicago Style recommendations. Double asterisks mark those differences.

16. Other Basic Facts

16.1: Publisher & Date for Books

Editions—editions other than the first should be noted after the title in simplified form.

Place (for books published before 2000)**—conventionally this is the city in which the publishing firm has headquarters, but may indicate the printer. Give the first place listed on the title page only. If there is ambiguity about the location (especially when it is not clarified by the name of the publisher), an abbreviation for the state or country should follow the place name. This requirement may have been useful in the past, but has become outdated. Dropping this requirement for books published since the year 2000 is strongly recommended.

Publisher

♦ Simplify the publisher's name but do not translate it.

♦ If there is no publisher listed, put "n.p."

Year of Publication

♦ Dates of publication are found either on the title page or copyright page.

♦ An "impression" or a "printing" is not a new edition.

♦ When possible, give the original year of publication for the first edition in brackets after the date for a later edition.

♦ If there is no year of publication listed, put "n.d."

16.2: Publisher & Date for Periodicals (Journals, Magazines, & Newspapers)

Treat All Periodicals in the Same Way **

Give the Periodical Title

Volume & Number—add the volume and issue number in Arabic numerals when listed on the title page. Precede the issue number with *no.* (for issue number). On the other hand, *vol.* (for volume) is rarely necessary.

Date—add the date of publication in as much detail as possible and in this order: day, month or season, year.

16.3: Publisher & Date for Internet Sources

Publisher—identify the organization that supports the site. This usually requires additional browsing.

Date—establish the date of composition and the most recent update.

Access Dates—do not list unless required.

Database—cite the name of a database in the bibliography only. **

16.4: Further Specifications

Page Numbers etc.

◆ Avoid using *p.* or *pp.* (for page or pages).

◆ Sections and Columns can be abbreviated in notes as *sec.* and *col.*

Note Numbers

◆ Cite foot- or endnotes in a source by giving the page number followed by *n.* (or plural, *nn.*) and then the note number.

Illustrations

◆ Cite illustrations by giving the page number first, then the type of illustration (plates, tables, maps, or figures), followed by the illustration number. Abbreviate illustration as *ill.* and figure as *fig.*

Web Site Information in Bibliography Only **

◆ Uniform Resource Locators (URLs) and Digital Object Identifiers (DOIs) are the strings of characters that designate specific locations on the internet

◆ Give the shortest form possible (URLs can often be shortened)

◆ For websites that can be searched, such as databases, give only the home or search page (or if preferred, a stable URL).

◆ Double-check for accuracy by searching by the exact URL or DOI.

◆ Use normal formatting (without underlining and in black ink).

◆ Do not use periods or other punctuation after the URL or DOI.

◆ Do not include retrieval information (i.e., lists of links to click).

◆ Use hyperlinks (or links) in digital papers.

16.5: Medium (if unusual)

For now, the word "paper" need not follow books and articles. But all unusual sources (e.g., material on CD-roms or DVDs) should note the medium in which they are stored or transmitted, if not otherwise clear, in the bibliography only.

---

17. Footnotes

17.1: Format

Insert sequential reference numbers for each footnote at the end of clauses, sentences, or paragraphs.

Only one note number at a time (never: 1, 2, 3).

The number should be in superscript, i.e. in a raised smaller font.

Footnotes are listed at the bottom of the page and start with the note number (in superscript or normal font).

Indent the first line of the footnote 0.25 inches.

Do not use endnotes (unless required). **

17a. Short Note Citations: Author & Title or Ibid.

After the first full citation in a note, the same source should be cited in shortened form. To shorten, choose either the Author & Title form or Ibid.

Author & Title. Use last names for authors and key words or phrases for short note citations. Eliminate other basic facts except page numbers and other specifications. Be consistent and be careful as similar authors or titles may require slightly longer citations for clarity.

Ibid. While Latin terms are generally no longer used in note citations, the abbreviation for *ibidem* (meaning "in the same place") is an exception. Ibid. indicates that the same author, title, and page(s) referenced in the previous note apply again. If you use Ibid., remember to capitalize the first letter and add the period. The abbreviation is usually not italicized. If necessary, add a comma followed by the appropriate page numbers or further specifications. Readers prefer Author & Title citations because this avoids the inconvenience of an Ibid. reference forcing them to turn back to a previous page.

Models

  3. Robert Sean Riley, *History of the Ditto Family*, 1700–2000, 2nd ed. (n.p., 1996), 10.

  4. Riley, *Ditto Family*, 15.

or

  4. Ibid., 15.

17.2: First References

The first time a source is introduced in the footnotes, the author and title must be cited in full.

Abbreviate editor and translator as ed. and trans., and give initials instead of first names.

Abbreviate other basic facts. **

Include publisher and date where known.

17.3: Subsequent Short References

After the first reference, the same source in the footnotes must be cited in a shortened form.

Short footnote citations should be as brief and unambiguous as possible.

More than one work by the same author, or similar titles, may require slightly longer short references for clarity.

Names may be shortened to last name only.

Titles may be shortened to a word or phrase.

Other basic facts are shortened to page numbers or other specifications.

On the use of Ibid., *see* 17a. Short Note Citations, *page 52.*

Shorten subsequent references to poems, plays, and ancient sources according to established conventions. *See* 17b *box at right.*

17.4: Combine Sources in One Note

One footnote may include citations for different sources.

Use semi-colons rather than periods to separate citations to multiple sources in one footnote.

Cite sources in the order they appear in the text.

Repeated references to one source are often best cited in one note at the end of the paragraph.

17b. Short References to Poems, Plays, & Ancient Sources

Shorten second citations to well known sources after the first full citation according to established conventions.

Bible: Give the abbreviated book title, chapter and verse(s): Gen. 2:9; Matt. 5:38–39

Plays: Give the short title, act, scene, and line(s): *Hamlet* 2.2.303–12; *Macbeth* 5.5.19–28

Ancient Texts: Give the short title, book or section and line(s): *Iliad* 23.382; *Odyssey* 3.24.

17.5: Additional Information in Notes

Explanatory (aka substantive, content, or discursive) **Notes**—brief explanations of important information, especially about sources, may be included in notes.

Quotations in Notes—source citation follows the final punctuation of each quotation and does not need to be in parentheses.

"See" & "See also"—use *see* or *see also* before source citations that are either broadly relevant to the point or that follow an explanation.

"But see" or "Compare"—use *but see* or *compare* (or its Latin abbreviation, cf.) to indicate sources that contradict or call into question the point of the note.

Latin Abbreviations—for idem, op. cit., loc. cit., and other esoterica [*see* 11a. Latin Terms and Abbreviations, *page 39*].

> ### 17c. Differences between Footnotes & Bibliographic Entries
>
> 1. The three sections of a citation (author, title, and other basic facts) are divided by commas in a footnote and by periods in a bibliographic entry. Note that in footnotes, other basic facts are placed in parentheses.
>
> 2. Footnotes are numbered; bibliographic entries are in alphabetical order.
>
> 3. Author names in bibliographies start with family names, while notes begin with first names.
>
> 4. Abbreviations are acceptable in notes, but not in bibliographic entries. **
>
> 5. Footnotes usually refer to a specific page or pages; bibliographic entries give no page numbers for books, and only inclusive page numbers for articles and parts of books.

18. Bibliographies

18.1: Format

The bibliography lists all of the materials consulted in the process of preparing the paper (including all sources cited in the footnotes) in alphabetical order.

Begin at the top of a separate page at the end of the paper.

Indent all but the first line of each bibliographic entry by 0.25 inches.

The bibliography should be titled by type.

Types

Bibliography—gives a comprehensive and unified list of sources relevant to the topic.

Selected Bibliography—lists only the sources cited in the notes.

Divided Bibliography—sectioned with subtitles either by topic or by classification of sources.

Annotated Bibliography—includes a brief description and evaluation of the source after every entry.

Bibliographic Essay—integrates the source citations into an essay on the variety and quality of sources available.

Further Reading—lists recommended sources.

19. Alphabetical Order in Bibliographies

19.1: General Principles

List the family name before the individual name (separated by a comma where the individual name is listed first as in the U.S., but not in cultures where the family name comes first).

Proceed letter-by-letter, not word by word. **

Put shorter names (and initials) before longer names.

Separate words at commas and parentheses, but ignore other punctuation.

19.2: Multiple Works by the Same Author or Authors

List single-author sources before multi-author ones.

List original before edited works.

List sources in either chronological order by date of publication or alphabetical order by title.

Using a three-em dash in place of the author's name in subsequent citations is not recommended. **

19.3: When there is no author or editor

Titles are ordered letter-by-letter.

Numbers in titles are ordered numeral-by-numeral in ascending order. **

Alphabetizing names can by tricky, particularly since it can be difficult to distinguish the individual name from the family name.

Principles

♦ In general, follow the author's preference or customary usage (it may be helpful to look up the author in a good biographical dictionary, library catalog, or database).

♦ When there is no clear precedent, simplify family names by putting traditional participles that are isolated by spaces (de, de la, le, van, von) after the individual name.

Ethnic Traditions—practices vary by culture, so the best practice is to research relevant traditions and follow established precedent. Two issues are common and examples give a taste of the complexities:

♦ *Patronymics & Matronymics*—kinship is often indicated by prefixes and the general rule is to include the prefix and to alphabetize letter by letter. For example, with Gaelic family names that begin with *M'*, *Mac*, or *Mc* (meaning *son of*) or O' (meaning *grandson*) ignore the apostrophe and then alphabetize. Similarly, with separate words that indicate kinship—such as in Arabic *ibn* and *bin* (meaning son of), *bint* (daughter of), *abu-* (father of), *umm* (mother of) or the Hebrew *ben* (son of) and *bat* (daughter of)—the rule is to treat these as parts of a compound family name and alphabetize accordingly even when there is no hyphen. But note for Arabic the prefixes *al* or *el* (the) are not treated as part of the name in establishing alphabetical order.

♦ *Compound Names*—In Spain and Latin America, for example, the father's family name and then the mother's family name come after the individual name, sometimes with a connecting y (and), and the whole compound is treated as a family name. In Portuguese cultures, however, the tradition is to alphabetize only by the last listed name—but not by the terms *Filho* (son), *Júnior* (junior), *Neto* (grandson), or *Sobrinho* (nephew) that sometimes follow the family name.

♦ *Family Names First*—In countries such as China, Korea, Japan, and Vietnam, family names come first followed by the name of the individual. For authors from these countries, their name order is not changed in a bibliography; but Asian authors publishing in the west may well have changed their name order.

20. Documentation Checklist

20.1: Text

Are all sources introduced with a signal phrase at least once?

Are footnote numbers placed in superscript after punctuation?

20.2: Footnotes

Numbering

◆ Are all footnotes numbered sequentially from one?

First References

◆ Are the author, title and other basic facts cited for each source on its first appearance in the footnotes?

◆ Are other basic facts properly abbreviated?

Subsequent References

◆ Are references to each source shortened after the first reference?

20.3: Bibliography

Does every source cited in the footnotes appear as well in the bibliography?

Is the bibliography ordered alphabetically by author's last name or by the beginning of a title?

Are all web page references shortened as far as possible and formatted as normal text?

20a. FAQs on Documenting

Where do I need to add a footnote? Cite at least one source with a footnote wherever you present information in the paper. Summaries, paraphrases, and direct quotations require a footnote, as do illustrations, statistics, and other specific facts.

Do I need to footnote everything? Facts that are widely known and uncontroversial—such as specific dates or general statements—are called common knowledge and do not need to be cited. But since it is not always easy to tell which facts are in this category, err on the side of caution by asking for advice and citing sources for information that is essential to your argument.

Can a paper have too many footnotes? No, but if you have more than one in the same paragraph it might be possible to combine them in a single footnote.

Can two or more sources be in the same footnote? Yes. *See* 17. Footnotes, *page 52.*

Can a footnote be in the middle of a sentence? Yes, if necessary for precision, but usually better to put it at the end.

Can I copy a source from the bibliography and use it for a footnote? No. *See* 17c. Differences between Footnote and Bibliographic Entries, *box on page 54.*

How do I cite a source that is not covered in the examples? Here are three solutions: (1) Find an example of how another scholar has cited this source in a publication; (2) Consult a more comprehensive list of examples in a style guide, such as *The Chicago Manual of Style*; (3) Use the logic of source citation (author, title, and other basic facts) explained in v: Documenting to provide the necessary information following the format of a similar source. *See also* 37. For Documenting, *page 84.*

V: Examples of Source Citation

This section gives examples of common citations in bibliographic and note form.

- ◆ For each source in this section, the bibliographic form comes first; the footnote form follows and begins with a number.

- ◆ Remember, after the first reference to a source in the footnotes, subsequent references to the same source should be shortened.

---

21. Books

21.1: Single Author

Evans, Richard J. *In Defense of History*. American edition. New York: W. W. Norton, 1999 [1997].

    10. Richard J. Evans, *In Defense of History*, American ed. (NY: W. W. Norton, 1999), 46.

21.2: Multiple Authors

Appleby, Joyce, Lynn Hunt, and Margaret Jacob. *Telling the Truth about History*. New York: Norton, 1994.

    11. Joyce Appleby, Lynn Hunt, and Margaret Jacob, *Telling the Truth about History* (NY: Norton, 1994), 47.

21.3: Publisher & Date Only (Since 2000)

Hoffer, Peter. *Past Imperfect: Facts, Fictions, Fraud—American History from Bancroft and Parkman to Ambrose, Bellesiles, Ellis, and Goodwin*. Revised edition. Public Affairs, 2007 [2004].

    12. Peter Hoffer, *Past Imperfect: Facts, Fictions, Fraud—American History from Bancroft and Parkman to Ambrose, Bellesiles, Ellis, and Goodwin*, rev. ed. (Public Affairs, 2007), 49.

21.4: Editor

Carnes, Mark C., editor. *Past Imperfect: History According to the Movies.* New York: H. Holt, 1995.

13. Mark C. Carnes, ed., *Past Imperfect: History According to the Movies* (NY: H. Holt, 1995), 50.

21.5: Translator

Bloch, Marc. *The Historian's Craft.* Translated by Peter Putnam. New York: Knopf, 1953.

14. Marc Bloch, *The Historian's Craft*, trans. P. Putnam (NY: Knopf, 1953), 51.

21.6: Edition

Carr, E. H. *What is History? The George Macaulay Trevelyan Lectures Delivered in the University of Cambridge, January–March 1961.* Edited by R. W. Davies. Second edition. London: Macmillan, 1986 [1961].

15. E. H. Carr, *What is History? The George Macaulay Trevelyan Lectures Delivered in the University of Cambridge, January–March 1961*, ed. R.W. Davies, 2nd ed. (London: Macmillan, 1986), 52.

21.7: Volume

Nora, Pierre, editor. *Realms of Memory: The Construction of the French Past; Volume 3, Symbols.* English-Language edition. Edited by Lawrence D. Kritzman. Translated by Arthur Goldhammer. New York: Columbia University Press, 1998 [1992].

16. Pierre Nora, ed., *Realms of Memory: The Construction of the French Past; Vol. 3, Symbols*, English ed., ed. L. D. Kritzman, trans. A. Goldhammer (NY: Columbia University Pr., 1998), 53.

21.8: Online & Electronic Books

Cary, Henry, translator. *The Histories of Herodotus.* New York: D. Appleton, 1904. Google Books. books.google.com.

17. Henry Cary, trans., *The Histories of Herodotus* (NY: D. Appleton, 1904), 55.

Thucydides. *The History of the Peloponnesian War*. Translated by Richard Crawley. n.p., n.d. Project Gutenberg. www.gutenberg.org/ebooks/7142.

18. Thucydides, *The History of the Peloponnesian War*, trans. R. Crawley (n.p., n.d.).

Fyfe, W. H., translator. *Tacitus: The Histories, Volumes I and II*. Oxford: Clarendon Press, 1912. Kindle edition.

19. W. H. Fyfe, trans., *Tacitus: The Histories* (Oxford: Clarendon Pr., 1912), 1:3.

22. Parts of Books

22.1: Part of a Book with a Title

Scott, Joan. "Women's History." In *New Perspectives on Historical Writing*. Edited by Peter Burke. University Park: The Pennsylvania State University Press, 1992 [1991], 42–66.

17. Joan Scott, "Women's History," in *New Perspectives on Historical Writing*, ed. P. Burke (University Park: Penn. State University Pr., 1992), 54.

22.2: Common Part of a Book

Trevor-Roper, H. R. Introduction. In *On History and Historians*, by Jacob Burkhardt. Translated by Harry Zohn. New York: Harper & Row, 1965 [1958], xi–xxi.

18. H. R. Trevor-Roper, Introduction, in *On History and Historians*, by Jacob Burkhardt, trans. H. Zohn (NY: Harper & Row, 1965), xv.

22.3: Article in a Reference Work

Butterfield, Herbert. "Historiography." In *Dictionary of the History of Ideas: Studies of Selected Pivotal Ideas*, volume 2. Edited by Philip P. Wiener. New York: Charles Scribner's Sons, 1973, 464–98.

19. Herbert Butterfield, "Historiography," in *Dictionary of the History of Ideas: Studies of Selected Pivotal Ideas*, vol. 2, ed. P. P. Wiener (NY: Charles Scribner's Sons, 1973), 475.

23. Articles & Reviews

23.1: From a Print Periodical (Journal, Magazine, or Newspaper)

Saunt, Claudio. "Telling Stories: The Political Uses of Myth and History in the Cherokee and Creek Nations." *The Journal of American History* 93, no. 3 (December 2006): 673–97.

20. Claudio Saunt, "Telling Stories: The Political Uses of Myth and History in the Cherokee and Creek Nations," *The Journal of American History* 93, no. 3 (Dec. 2006): 675.

23.2: From a Periodical in an Online Database

Rosenfeld, Gavriel. "Why Do We Ask 'What if?' Reflections on the Function of Alternate History." *History and Theory* 41, no. 4 (December 2002): 90–103. JSTOR. www.jstor.org [or if preferred: www.jstor.org/stable/3590670].

21. Gavriel Rosenfeld, "Why Do We Ask 'What if?' Reflections on the Function of Alternate History," *History and Theory* 41, no. 4 (Dec. 2002): 95.

23.3: Book Review

Munro, Doug. Review of *What Is History Now?* Edited by David Cannadine. *Journal of Social History* 37, no. 3 (2004): 814–16. JSTOR. www.jstor.org [or if preferred: www.jstor.org/stable/3790184]

22. Doug Munro, review of *What Is History Now?* ed. D. Cannadine. *Journal of Social History* 37, no. 3 (2004): 815.

23.4: Movie Review

Holden, Stephen. "From the Stage to the Screen, History Worth Repeating." Review of *The History Boys* (2006), directed by Nicholas Hytner. *New York Times* (21 November 2006).

23. Stephen Holden, "From the Stage to the Screen, History Worth Repeating," review of *The History Boys* (2006), *The New York Times* (21 Nov. 2006).

24. Websites & Discussion Lists

Online and Electronic Books and Articles are discussed on pages 60–61.

24.1: Web Site with Author or Editor

Censer, Jack, and Lynn Hunt. *Liberty, Equality, and Fraternity: Exploring the French Revolution*. Center for History and New Media, George Mason University, 2001. chnm.gmu.edu/revolution

30. Jack Censer and Lynn Hunt, *Liberty, Equality, and Fraternity: Exploring the French Revolution* (Center for History and New Media, George Mason University, 2001).

24.2: Web Site without Author or Editor

History.com. The History Channel.

31. *History.com* (The History Channel).

24.3: Web Page on a Web Site

"Abolitionists Rampant," *Valley Spirit* (1 January 1862), 4 col. 2. In *Valley of the Shadow: Two Communities in the American Civil War*. Virginia Center for Digital History, University of Virginia. valley.vcdh.virginia.edu

31. "Abolitionists Rampant," *Valley Spirit* (1 Jan. 1862), 4 col. 2, in *Valley of the Shadow: Two Communities in the American Civil War* (Virginia Center for Digital History, University of Virginia).

24.4: Web Log (Blog)

MacDougall, Rob. "The Further Adventures of Ben Franklin's Ghost," 8 November 2007. *Cliopatria: A Group Blog*. History News Network, George Mason University. hnn.us/blogs/entries/44468.html.

32. Rob MacDougall, "The Further Adventures of Ben Franklin's Ghost," 8 Nov. 2007, *Cliopatria: A Group Blog* (HNN, George Mason University).

24.5: Discussion List Posting

Martini, Edwin. "Two Articles on The Return of SDS," 5 March 2007. H-1960s, H-Net, Michigan State University. www.h-net.org/~h-1960s.

33. Edwin Martini, "Two Articles on The Return of SDS," 5 Mar. 2007 (H-1960s, H-Net, Mich. State University).

25. Recorded Sounds, Videos, & Images

25.1: Sound Recording

Ledbetter, Huddie. *Leadbelly's Last Sessions.* Smithsonian Folkways, 1994. CD.

40. Huddie Ledbetter, "Nobody in This World is Better Than Us," on *Leadbelly's Last Sessions* (Smithsonian Folkways, 1994).

25.2: Video Recording

Howard Zinn: You Can't Be Neutral on a Moving Train. Directed by Deb Ellis and Denis Mueller. First Run Features, 2005. DVD

41. Howard Zinn, "Speech at Veterans for Peace Conference 2004," on *Howard Zinn: You Can't Be Neutral on a Moving Train*, dir. D. Ellis and D. Mueller (First Run Features, 2005).

25.3: Artwork or Image

Gentileschi, Artemisia. *Judith and Her Maidservant.* Oil on canvas, c.1625. The Detroit Institute of Arts.

42. Artemisia Gentileschi, *Judith and Her Maidservant* (c.1625).

25.4: Online Multimedia

Christian, David. "The History of Our World in 18 Minutes." TED, 2011. Video. www.ted.com/talks/david_christian_big_history.html.

43. David Christian, "The History of Our World in 18 Minutes" (TED, 2011).

26. Oral Sources

26.1: Lecture

Fanelli, Doris. "Race and Slavery at the Liberty Bell." Lecture, Old South Meeting House, Boston, 20 September 2006. WGBH Forum Network. dev.forum-network.org/lecture/dorris-fanelli-race-and-slavery-liberty-bell.

50. Doris Fanelli, "Race and Slavery at the Liberty Bell," lecture, Old South Meeting House, Boston (20 Sep. 2006).

26.2: Text of a Speech

Pinter, Harold. "Art, Truth, and Politics." Nobel Lecture. Stockholm, 7 December 2005. Nobelprize.org. nobelprize.org/nobel_prizes/literature/laureates/2005/pinter-lecture-e.html.

51. Harold Pinter, "Art, Truth, and Politics," Nobel Lecture (Stockholm, 7 Dec. 2005).

26.3: Podcast

Mandela, Nelson. "Address Upon Release From Prison." *Great Speeches in History Podcast*. LearnOutLoud.com. www.learnoutloud.com/Audio-Books/Politics/Political-Figures/Nelson-Mandela--Address-Upon-Release-from-Prison/24126.

52. Nelson Mandela, "Address Upon Release From Prison," *Great Speeches in History Podcast*.

26.4: Oral Interview

Alley, Jesse L., Jr. Interview with John R. Milam, 10 November 2005. Recording, Jesse L. Alley, Jr. Collection, The Vietnam Archive, Texas Tech University. www.vietnam.ttu.edu/oralhistory/interviews/browse/oha.php.

53. Jesse L. Alley, Jr., interview with J. R. Milam, 10 Nov. 2005 (recording, Jesse L. Alley, Jr. Collection, The Vietnam Archive, Texas Tech University).

26.5: Published Interview

Terkel, Studs. "*PW* Talks with Studs Terkel: A Working Life." *Publishers Weekly* 254, no. 38 (24 September 2007): 54.

24. Studs Terkel, "*PW* Talks with Studs Terkel: A Working Life," *Publishers Weekly* 254, no. 38 (24 Sep. 2007): 54.

---

27. Theses & Dissertations

Brown, Bradford C. "Kingship and the French Revolution of 1830: The Meaning of Royal Authority in Popular Political Culture and Orléanism." PhD dissertation. University of California Santa Barbara, June 1999.

60. Bradford C. Brown, "Kingship and the French Revolution of 1830: The Meaning of Royal Authority in Popular Political Culture and Orléanism" (PhD diss., University of Calif. Santa Barbara, June 1999), 55.

---

28. Government and Legal Documents

The Chicago Manual of Style recommends using the latest edition of either *The Bluebook: A Uniform System of Citation* or *ALWD Citation Manual: A Professional System of Citation.*

See also Diane L. Garner and Diane H. Smith, eds., *The Complete Guide to Citing Government Information Resources: A Manual for Writers and Librarians*, rev. ed. (Bethesda, MD: American Library Association, 1993).

For quick practical help, see the list of "Guides to Citing Government and Legal Documents." *See* VII: Internet Resources, *page 73.*

29. Sources in Collections

Published documents are usually treated as Books or Parts of Books. Unpublished documents from archival collections are cited by author, title, and other basic facts (including collection) in footnotes, but only the collection is listed in the bibliography (usually in a separate section of a Divided Bibliography). If the document is from a private collection, it may be necessary to title the collection and to add contact information in the bibliographic citation.

29.1: Published Letters

Garrison, William Lloyd. *The Letters of William Lloyd Garrison, Vol. III: No Union With Slave-Holders, 1841–1849*, edited by Walter M. Merrill. Cambridge: Belknap Press, 1973.

70. William Lloyd Garrison to Parker Pillsbury, 23 Feb. 1841, Boston, in *The Letters of William Lloyd Garrison, Vol. III: No Union With Slave-Holders, 1841–1849*, ed. W. M. Merrill (Cambridge: Belknap Press, 1973), 14–16.

29a. Source Quoted in Another Source

The best practice, when possible, is to track down the original source. Note that both sources are listed in the footnote only.

Southgate, Beverley. *Why Bother with History? Ancient, Modern, and Postmodern Motivations*. Longman, 2000.

73. William Morris, "How I Became a Socialist," *Justice* (16 June 1894), quoted in Beverley Southgate, *Why Bother with History? Ancient, Modern, and Postmodern Motivations* (Longman, 2000), 65.

29.2: **Unpublished Letters**

Lafayette Collection, Division of Rare and Manuscripts, Cornell University Library. rmc.library.cornell.edu/lafayette/collection.

71. Lafayette to Adrienne de Noailles de Lafayette, Charleston, 15 June 1777, Lafayette Collection, Cornell University Library.

29.3: **Other Archival Documents**

American Memory. The Library of Congress. memory.loc.gov/ammem/index.html.

72. "Breaker boys, Woodward Coal Mines, Kingston, Pa." [photograph], LC-D401-11590, Detroit Publishing Company Collection, Prints and Photographs Division, *American Memory* (The Library of Congress).

30. Sample First Page and Bibliography

One-inch margins all around

Jousting Over the Decline of the Knights of Labor
History 350: Historical Methods
Courtney Wiersema
17 April 2007

Single-space the heading

Double-space the text

1886 was a watershed year in American labor history marked by organization and conflict, hopes for a better life and the realities of violence. The Knights of Labor were undeniably the key players in this dramatic year. Their sudden disappearance from prominence in the years after 1886 though is puzzling. Historians continue to disagree vehemently about whether the decline was caused by external forces or internal factors and if the implications of decline were advantageous or limiting.

Five historians have addressed this issue over the last thirty years. In *The Making of American Exceptionalism*, Kim Voss uses a case study of the New Jersey Knights of Labor to argue that the strength of American employer opposition kept the labor movement from succeeding.[1] Focusing on strikes and organization in Sedalia, Missouri, Michael Cassity writes about the complexities of modernization in shaping the movement.[2] Cassity concludes that the Knights' downfall came from their errant ideological focus on the political and the distant, rather than the local and the specific.[3] In another study, Susan Levine asks some big questions about the

Note number at end of sentence

Shorten note after first citation

Footnotes at bottom of page

[1] Kim Voss, *The Making of American Exceptionalism: The Knights of Labor and Class Formation in the Nineteenth Century* (Ithaca: Cornell University Press, 1993), 202.

[2] Michael Cassity, "Modernization and Social Crisis: The Knights of Labor and a Midwest Community, 1885–1886," *The Journal of American History* 66, no. 1 (June 1979): 41–61.

[3] Cassity, "Modernization," 43.

Specific page number

Last name first

Bibliography

12

Page numbers starting on page 2

Cassity, Michael J. "Modernization and Social Crisis: The Knights of Labor and a Midwest Community, 1885–1886." *The Journal of American History* 66, no. 1 (June 1979): 41–61.

Fink, Leon. "The New Labor History and the Powers of Historical Pessimism: Consensus, Hegemony and the Case of the Knights of Labor." *The Journal of American History* 75, no. 1 (June 1988): 115–36.

Kaufman, Jason. "Rise and Fall of a Nation of Joiners: The Knights of Labor Revisited." *Journal of Interdisciplinary History* 31, no. 4 (Spring 2001): 553–79.

Levine, Susan. "Labor's True Woman: Domesticity and Equal Rights in the Knights of Labor." *The Journal of American History* 70, no. 2 (September 1983): 323–39.

Voss, Kim. The Making of American Exceptionalism: *The Knights of Labor and Class Formation in the Nineteenth Century*. Ithaca: Cornell University Press, 1993

Page range

Alphabetical order

Indent after first line

VI: Further Reading

31. Guides for History Students

Abbot, Mary, ed. *History Skills: A Student's Handbook*. Second edition. Routledge, 2009.

Barzun, Jacques, and Henry F. Graff. *The Modern Researcher*. Sixth edition. Wadsworth, 2003.

Benjamin, Jules R. *A Student's Guide to History*. Eleventh edition. Bedford/ St. Martin's, 2009.

Booth, Wayne C., Gregory G. Colomb, and Joseph M. Williams. *The Craft of Research*. Third edition. University of Chicago Press, 2008.

Brundage, Anthony. *Going to the Sources: A Guide to Historical Research and Writing*. Fourth edition. Harlan Davidson, 2007.

Cullen, Jim. *Essaying the Past: How to Read, Write, and Think about History*. Wiley-Blackwell, 2009.

Fisher, Steven, ed. *Archival Information: How to Find It, How to Use It*. Greenwood, 2004.

Frakes, Robert. *Writing for College History*. Houghton Mifflin, 2004.

Fritze, Ronald H., Brian E. Coutts, Louis Andrew Vyhnanek. *Reference Sources in History: An Introductory Guide*. Second edition. ABC-CLIO, 2004.

Galgano, Michael J., Raymond M. Hyser, and J. Christopher Arndt. *Doing History: Research and Writing in the Digital Age*. Second edition. Cengage, 2012.

Gregory, Ian N. *A Place in History: A Guide to Using GIS in Historical Research*. Oxbow, 2003.

Howell, Martha, and Walter Prevenier. *From Reliable Sources: An Introduction to Historical Methods*. Cornell University Press, 2001.

McDowell, W. H. *Historical Research: A Guide for Writers of Dissertations, Theses, Articles, and Books*. Longman, 2002.

Marius, Richard, and Melvin E. Page. *A Short Guide to Writing about History*. Eighth edition. Pearson Longman, 2011.

Mills, Elizabeth Shown. *Evidence Explained: Citing History Sources from Artifacts to Cyberspace*. Second edition. Genealogical Publishing, 2009.

Presnell, Jenny L. *The Information-Literate Historian: A Guide to Research for History Students*. New York: Oxford University Press, 2007.

Rampolla, Mary Lynn. *A Pocket Guide to Writing in History*. Seventh edition. Bedford/St. Martin's, 2012.

Storey, William Kelleher. *Writing History: A Guide for Students*. Third edition. Oxford University Press, 2009.

Williams, Robert C. *The Historian's Toolbox: A Student's Guide to the Theory and Craft of History*. Third Edition. M. E. Sharpe, 2011.

32. Guides to Writing Style

Aaron, Jane E. *The Little, Brown Essential Handbook*. Twelfth edition. Addison Wesley, 2012.

Anson, Chris M., Robert A. Schwegler, and Marcia F. Muth. *The Longman Pocket Writer's Companion*. Third edition. Pearson Longman, 2011.

Faigley, Lester. *The Brief Penguin Handbook*. Fourth edition. Addison Wesley, 2012.

Hacker, Diana, and Nancy Sommers. *A Pocket Style Manual*. Sixth edition. Bedford St. Martin's, 2011.

Maimon, Elaine P., Janice H. Peritz, and Kathleen Blake Yancey. *A Writer's Resource*. Third edition. McGraw Hill, 2010.

MLA Handbook for Writers of Research Papers. Seventh edition. MLA, 2009.

The Chicago Manual of Style: The Essential Guide for Writers, Editors, and Publishers. Sixteenth edition. The University of Chicago Press, 2010.

Turabian, Kate. *A Manual for Writers of Term Papers, Theses, and Dissertations*. Eighth edition. The University of Chicago Press, 2013.

33. Writing on Writing

Barzun, Jacques. *Simple and Direct: A Rhetoric for Writers*. Fourth edition. Harper Collins, 2001.

Lanham, Richard. *Revising Prose*. Fifth edition. Pearson Longman, 2007.

Strunk, William, Jr., and E. B. White. *The Elements of Style*. Fiftieth anniversary edition. Longman, 2008.

Williams, Joseph M. *Style: Lessons in Clarity and Grace*. Tenth edition. Pearson Longman, 2010.

Zinsser, William. *On Writing Well: The Classic Guide to Writing Nonfiction*. Thirtieth anniversary edition. Harper Collins, 2006.

34. History of Documentation

Anderson, B. "The Decline and Fall of Footnotes." *Stanford Magazine* (January-February 1997), www.stanfordalumni.org/news/magazine/1997/janfeb/articles/footnotes.html.

Grafton, Anthony. *The Footnote: A Curious History*. Cambridge: Harvard University Press, 1999.

Zerby, Chuck. *The Devil's Details: A History of the Footnote*. Simon & Schuster, 2003.

VII: Internet Resources

These selected categories and resources should not be taken as the last word or link. Sites and pages are listed for ease of use, but not cited as in a bibliography.

35. For Researching

35.1: Evaluating Internet Resources

- Evaluation of Information Sources, ed. Alistair Smith (WWW Virtual Library): www.vuw.ac.nz/staff/alastair_smith/evaln/evaln.htm
- Finding Scholarly Content on the Web by Laura Cohen (Internet Tutorials): www.internettutorials.net/finding-scholarly-content.asp
- Internet Detective (Intute): www.vtstutorials.ac.uk/detective

35.2: General Reference

- Answers.com: www.answers.com
- Bartleby: www.bartleby.com
- Biography Index: www.ebscohost.com/academic/biography-index-past-and-present
- Encyclopedia Britannica Online: www.britannica.com
- Encyclopedia.com: www.encyclopedia.com
- Gale Virtual Reference Library (subscription): www.gale.cengage.com/servlet/GvrlMS?msg=ma
- Refdesk: www.refdesk.com
- Virtual Reference Shelf, Library of Congress: www.loc.gov/rr/askalib/virtualref.html
- Wikipedia: en.wikipedia.org

35.3: Gateways, Portals, & Subject Directories

General Academic

◆ Best of the Web: botw.org

◆ BUBL Link: bubl.ac.uk

◆ Infomine: infomine.ucr.edu

◆ Internet Public Library 2: www.ipl.org

◆ Internet Scout Project Archives: scout.wisc.edu/Archives/index.php

◆ Intute: www.intute.ac.uk

◆ Open Directory Project: www.dmoz.org

◆ WWW Virtual Library: vlib.org

General History (including links to primary sources)

◆ Best of History Websites (EdTechTeacher): www.besthistorysites.net

◆ BUBL Link, History, General Resources (Centre for Digital Library Research, Strathclyde University): bubl.ac.uk/link/linkbrowse.cfm?menuid=11369

◆ CHNM—Center for History and New Media (Department of History and Art History, George Mason University): chnm.gmu.edu.

◆ Digital History by S. Mintz and S. McNeil (University of Houston): www.digitalhistory.uh.edu

◆ Digital Librarian, History: www.digital-librarian.com/history.html

◆ Digital Library for the Decorative Arts and Materical Culture (University of Wisconsin, Madison): decorativearts.library.wisc.edu

◆ eHistory (Department of History, The Ohio State University): ehistory.osu.edu/osu

◆ Guide to Internet Resources for Historians, Cromohs (Firenze University Press): www.cromohs.unifi.it/eng

◆ Historical Text Archive, ed. Don Mabry: historicaltextarchive.com

◆ History Central Catalogue, WWW Virtual Library (European University Institute, Florence): vlib.iue.it/history/index.html

- History Guide, Library of Anglo-American Culture and History (Göttingen State and University Library): aac.sub.uni-goettingen.de/en/history/guide/info

- History On-Line (Institute of Historical Research, University of London): www.history.ac.uk/ihr/Resources

- History World: www.historyworld.net

- Online History Degree Programs & Schools, Academic Info: www.academicinfo.net/hist.html

- Resources for Historians, History Guide: www.historyguide.org/resources.html

- Student's Online Guide to History Reference Sources by Jules R. Benjamin (Bedford/St. Martin's): bcs.bedfordstmartins.com/benjamin11e

- Voice of the Shuttle, History (University of California Santa Barbara): vos.ucsb.edu.

- World Digital Library, UNESCO: www.wdl.org/en

- World History Compass: www.worldhistorycompass.com

- Yahoo! History: dir.yahoo.com/Arts/Humanities/History

35.4: Primary Sources

See also 35.3: Gateways, Portals, & Subject Directories, *page 74, and* 35.9: Archives & Museums, *page 80.*

Using & Evaluating Primary Sources

- Analyzing Documents, World History Matters (CHNM, George Mason University): chnm.gmu.edu/worldhistorysources/whmdocuments.html

- Guide to Doing History with Objects by S. Lubar and K. Kendrick, The Object of History (CHNM, George Mason University): objectofhistory.org/guide

- Making Sense of Evidence, [U.S.] History Matters (CHNM, George Mason University): historymatters.gmu.edu/browse/makesense

- Unpacking Evidence, World History Matters (CHNM, George Mason University): chnm.gmu.edu/worldhistorysources/whmunpacking.html

- Using Primary Sources on the Web (RUSA, American Library Association): www.ala.org/rusa/sections/history/resources/pubs/usingprimarysources

- What are Primary Sources? Primary Sources at Yale (Yale University): www.yale.edu/collections_collaborative/primarysources/primarysources.html

Portals, Collections, & Digital Libraries

General

- ACLS Humanities E-Book Project [subscription]: www.humanitiesebook.org

- Art History Resources by Christopher L.C.E. Whitcombe: arthistoryresources.net/ARTHLinks.html

- Avalon Project: Documents in Law, History, and Diplomacy (Lillian Goldman Law Library, Yale University): avalon.law.yale.edu

- Collaborative Digital Libraries (Library of Cognress): international.loc.gov/intldl/find/digital_collaborations.html

- Digital Collections [books, manuscripts, documents, and artworks 1400s-present] (Getty Research Institute): www.getty.edu/research/tools/digital_collections

- Digital Collections (Library of Congress): international.loc.gov/intldl/find/digital_collections.html

- Eyewitness to History (IBIS): www.eyewitnesstohistory.com/index.html.

- Google Books: books.google.com

- Hanover Historical Texts Collection (Hanover College): history.hanover.edu/project.php

- History Studies Centre, Proquest [subscription]: www.historystudycentre.co.uk

- In the First Person: Index to Letters, Diaries, Oral Histories, and Personal Narratives (Alexander Street Press): www.inthefirstperson.com/firp

- Internet History Sourcebooks Project, ed. Paul Halsall (Fordham University): www.fordham.edu/Halsall/index.asp

- List of Digital Library Projects, Wikipedia: en.wikipedia.org/wiki/List_of_digital_library_projects

- Online Books Page, ed. John Mark Ockerbloom (University of Pennsylvania): digital.library.upenn.edu/books

- Online Primary Sources, ed. Kathryn Otto (Society of American Archivists): nhdarchives.pbworks.com/w/page/37998731/Online%20Primary%20Sources

- Perseus Digital Library, ed. Gregory R. Crane (Tufts University): www.perseus.tufts.edu/hopper/collections

- Primary Documents Online, ed. Judith A. Downie (Cal. State University San Marcos): library.csusm.edu/subject_guides/history/online_primary.asp

- Primary Sources Online by Carolyn Paul Branch: primarysourcesonline.com/welcome.html

- Project Gutenberg [digital library]: www.gutenberg.org

- Questia [for-pay digital library with some free content]: www.questia.com.

- Swarthmore College Peace Collection: www.swarthmore.edu/library/peace

- Web Gallery of Art: www.wga.hu

- Web Resources for Art, Art History and Archaeology (University Libraries, University of Maryland): www.lib.umd.edu/guides/artinternet.html

U.S. History

- AMDOCS: Documents for the Study of American History, ed. George Laughead (WWW Virtual Library): www.vlib.us/amdocs

- American Memory (Library of Congress): memory.loc.gov

- Many Pasts, [U.S.] History Matters (CHNM, George Mason University): historymatters.gmu.edu/browse/manypasts

- U.S. History Digital Library (Academic Info): www.academicinfo.net/histuslibrary.html

- U.S. History, [Other] Primary Source Collections (Library of Congress): www.loc.gov/teachers/additionalresources/relatedresources/ushist/primary.html

35.5: Library Catalogs

World

- Libdex: www.libdex.com
- Libweb: www.lib-web.org
- WorldCat: www.worldcat.org
- The European Library: www.theeuropeanlibrary.org

U.S. Libraries and Archives

- Center for Research Libraries—an international consortium: www.crl.edu
- Library of Congress—the largest library in the world, the LOC receives copies of every publication made or distrbuted in the U.S.: www.loc.gov
- University Libraries—a list of the 20 largest in the U.S. with links to their catalog systems, see ALA Library Fact Sheet Number 22 (2011), www.ala.org:

    1. University of California (combined): melvyl.worldcat.org
    2. Harvard University: library.harvard.edu
    3. University of Illinois, Urbana-Champaign: www.library.uiuc.edu
    4. Yale University: www.library.yale.edu
    5. Columbia University: library.columbia.edu
    6. University of Texas: www.lib.utexas.edu
    7. University of Michigan: www.lib.umich.edu
    8. University of Chicago: www.lib.uchicago.edu
    9. Indiana University: www.libraries.iub.edu
    10. Stanford University: library.stanford.edu
    11. University of Wisconsin: www.library.wisc.edu
    12. Cornell University: www.library.cornell.edu
    13. University of Washington: catalog.wustl.edu
    14. Princeton University: catalog.princeton.edu
    15. University of Minnesota: umnlib.oit.umn.edu/F
    16. University of North Carolina: www.lib.unc.edu
    17. University of Pennsylvania: www.library.upenn.edu

18. Ohio State University: library.osu.edu
19. Duke University: library.duke.edu
20. University of Pittsburgh: www.library.pitt.edu

35.6: Library Classification Guides

◆ Library of Congress Classification: www.loc.gov/catdir/cpso/lcco

◆ Dewey Decimal: www.oclc.org/dewey/resources/summaries

35.7: Databases for Articles, Dissertations, & More [Subscription]

Articles

◆ Academic OneFile: www.gale.cengage.com/PeriodicalSolutions/academicOnefile.htm

◆ Academic Search Complete: www.ebscohost.com/academic/academic-search-complete

◆ America: History & Life: www.ebscohost.com/public/america-history-and-life

◆ FirstSearch: www.oclc.org/firstsearch

◆ Historical Abstracts: www.ebscohost.com/public/historical-abstracts

◆ History Cooperative: www.historycooperative.org

◆ Humanities Index: www.ebscohost.com/corporate-research/humanities-international-index

◆ JSTOR: www.jstor.org

◆ Lexis-Nexis Academic: www.lexisnexis.com/hottopics/lnacademic

◆ Project Muse: muse.jhu.edu

Book Reviews

◆ Book Review Digest Plus: www.ebscohost.com/academic/book-review-digest-plus

◆ Book Review Index Online: www.gale.cengage.com/BRIOnline

◆ H-Net Reviews: www.h-net.org/reviews

Chapters in Anthologies

◆ Essay and General Literature Index Retrospective, 1900–1984: www.ebscohost.com/academic/essay-and-general-literature-retrospective

Dissertations & Theses

◆ Networked Digital Library of Theses and Dissertations: www.ndltd.org

◆ ProQuest Dissertations & Theses Database: www.proquest.com/en-US/catalogs/databases/detail/pqdt.shtml

35.8: History Journals Directories

◆ Directory of History Journals [peer-reviewed journals in English] (AHA): www.historians.org/pubs/free/journals

◆ Directory of Open Access Journals, History: www.doaj.org/doaj

◆ History Journals Index, D'Història: www.uv.es/apons/revistes.htm

35.9: Archives & Museums

◆ Archive Finder (ProQuest): archives.chadwyck.com/marketing/index.jsp

◆ Archive Grid (OCLC): archivegrid.org/web/index.jsp

◆ Archives Made Easy (London School of Economics and Political Science): www.archivesmadeeasy.org

◆ International Council of Museums: icom.museum

◆ Museum of Museums: www.museumlink.com

◆ Repositories of Primary Sources: www.uiweb.uidaho.edu/special-collections/Other.Repositories.html

◆ Virtual Library Museums Pages: archives.icom.museum/vlmp

35.10: **Search Engines**

Directories

◆ Internet Tutorials: www.internettutorials.net/engines.asp

◆ Search Engine Colossus: www.searchenginecolossus.com

◆ Wikipedia: en.wikipedia.org/wiki/List_of_search_engines

General

◆ Ask: ask.com

◆ Clusty: clusty.com

◆ Google: google.com

Metasearch

◆ Dogpile: www.dogpile.com

◆ Harvester42: harvester42.fzk.de/jss/Search

◆ Ixquick: www.ixquick.com

◆ Webcrawler: webcrawler.com

Specialized

◆ Google by Country:
  wwp.greenwichmeantime.com/time-zone/europe/uk/google-uk

◆ Google Scholar: scholar.google.com

◆ iSEEK: education.iseek.com

35.11: **Note-taking Software Reviews**

◆ CNET—for reviews of specific software: www.cnet.com

◆ Comparison of Free Bibliographic Managers: mahbub.wordpress.
  com/2007/03/04/comparison-of-free-bibliographic-managers

◆ Comparison of Reference Management Software: en.wikipedia.
  org/wiki/Comparison_of_reference_management_software

◆ Reference Management Overview: blogs.plos.org/mfenner/
  reference-manager-overview

35.12: Discussion Lists & Blogs

- H-HistMajor—"a moderated internet discussion forum of, by, and for undergraduate history majors": www.h-net.org/~hstmajor

- H-Net: www.h-net.org

- History Blogs, Blog Catalog: www.blogcatalog.com/directory/history

- History, Academic Blogs Portal: academicblogs.org/index.php/History

- HNN Blogs: hnn.us/articles/1572.html

- HNN: hnn.us

35.13: Guides to Internet Resources

- Cohen, Laura. "Internet Tutorials": www.internettutorials.net

- Harnack, Andrew, and Eugene Kleppinger. *Online! A Reference Guide to Using Internet Sources*. 3rd ed. Bedford/St. Martin's, 2003.

- Lehner, Kristin, Kelly Schrum, and T. Mills Kelly. *World History Matters: A Student Guide to World History Online*. Bedford/St. Martin's, 2009.

- Reagan, Patrick. *Guide to History and the Internet*. McGraw-Hill, 2002.

- Schrum, Kelly, Alan Gevinson, and Roy Rosenzweig. *History Matters: A Student Guide to U.S. History Online*. Second edition. Bedford/St. Martin's, 2009.

- Trinkle, Dennis A., and Scott A. Merriman. *The American History Highway: A Guide to Internet Resources on U.S., Canadian and Latin American History*. M. E. Sharpe, 2007.

- Trinkle, Dennis A., and Scott A. Merriman. *The European History Highway: A Guide to Internet Resources*. M. E. Sharpe, 2002.

- Trinkle, Dennis A., and Scott A. Merriman. *The History Highway: A 21st-Century Guide to Internet Resources*. 4th ed. M. E. Sharpe, 2006.

- Trinkle, Dennis A., and Scott A. Merriman. *The World History Highway: A Guide to Internet Resources*. M. E. Sharpe, 2002.

36. For Writing

36.1: Guides to Composition

- Guide to Grammar and Style by Jack Lynch (Rutgers University, 2011): andromeda.rutgers.edu/~jlynch/Writing/contents.html

- The Elements of Style by William Strunk, Jr. (1918): www.bartleby.com/141/index.html

- Writer's Handbook (Writing Center, UW-Madison): www.wisc.edu/writing/Handbook/index.html.

36.2: Guides to Writing History Papers

- A Brief Guide to Writing the History Paper by Dan Wewers (Writing Center, Harvard College, 2007): isites.harvard.edu/fs/docs/icb.topic526630.files/BG%20Writing%20History.pdf

- A Student's Guide to the Study of History by Steven Kreis (2000): www.historyguide.org/guide/guide.html#Table

- Handouts, History Writing Resource Center (College of William & Mary, 2012): www.wm.edu/as/history/undergraduateprogram/historywritingresourcecenter/handouts

- How to Write a Research Paper in History, Wikibooks: en.wikibooks.org/wiki/How_to_Write_a_Research_Paper_in_History

- Reading, Writing, and Researching for History by Patrick Rael (Bowdoin College, 2004): academic.bowdoin.edu/WritingGuides

- Tips for Writing History Papers, History Department (Boston College, 2012): www.bc.edu/schools/cas/history/resources/tips.html

- Writing a Good History Paper, History Department (Hamilton College, 2008): www.hamilton.edu/documents/writing-center/WritingGoodHistoryPaper.pdf

- Writing the History Paper by Karen Gocsik (Dartmouth College, 2005): www.dartmouth.edu/~writing/materials/student/soc_sciences/history.shtml

37. For Documenting

37.1: Citation Engines

Although simple to use, citation engines are not always reliable so check the results.

- BibMe: www.bibme.org
- EasyBib (ImagineEasy Solutions): www.easybib.com
- KnightCite (Hekman Library, Calvin College): www.calvin.edu/library/knightcite
- Son of Citation Machine by David Warlick (The Landmark Project): citationmachine.net

37.2: CMS

- *The Chicago Manual of Style Online*, 16th ed. (The University of Chicago, 2010): www.chicagomanualofstyle.org/home.html

37.3: Short Guides to Chicago Style Citation

- *Chicago Manual of Style*, Online Writing Lab (Purdue University): owl.english.purdue.edu/owl/resource/717/01
- *Chicago-Style Citation Quick Guide*, CMS Online: www.chicagomanualofstyle.org/tools_citationguide.html
- *Chicago/Turabian Documentation*, The Writing Center (UW-Madison): writing.wisc.edu/Handbook/DocChicago.html
- *History: Documenting Sources* by D. Hacker and B. Fister, Research and Documentation Online, 5th ed. (Bedford/St Martin's): bcs.bedfordstmartins.com/resdoc5e/RES5e_ch10_o.html

37.4: Guides to Citing Internet & Electronic Sources

- *Citing Electronic Information in History Papers* by Maurice Crouse (The University of Memphis, 2011): cassian.memphis.edu/history/mcrouse/elcite.html
- *Citing Online Sources* by Michael B. Quinlon: www.worldwidewords.org/articles/citation.htm

Guides to Citing Government & Legal Documents

◆ *ALWD Citation Manual Resources* (Association of Legal Writing Directors): www.alwd.org/publications/citation_manual.html

◆ *Brief Guide to Citing Government Documents* (The University Libraries, University of Memphis): www.memphis.edu/govpub/ citweb.php

◆ *Citing Government Documents/Government Agency Style Manuals* (University of North Texas Libraries): www.library.unt.edu/ govinfo/browse-topics/citation-guides-and-style-manuals/ citing-government-documents

◆ *Citing Government Information Sources Using MLA Style*, (University Libraries, University of Nevada Reno): knowledgecen- ter.unr.edu/help/manage/government_cite.aspx

◆ *Guide to Citing Government Publications* (Indiana University Libraries): www.libraries.iub.edu/index.php?pageId=2558

◆ Introduction to Basic Legal Citation by Peter Martin: www.law. cornell.edu/citation

◆ *The Bluebook: A Uniform System of Citation*, 18th ed. (Harvard Law Review Association, 2005): www.legalbluebook.com

◆ *The University of Chicago Manual of Legal Citation* (The University of Chicago Law Review, 2013): lawreview.uchicago.edu/page/ maroonbook